UNFULFILLED PROPHECY
And The Hope of The Church

And

FORGOTTEN TRUTHS

Two Books

Sir Robert Anderson, LL.D.

Trumpet Press, Lawton, OK U.S.A.

Author: Anderson, Robert.

Title: UNFULFILLED PROPHECY And The Hope of The Church
1. Return of Christ 2. Rapture 3. Eschatology 4. Millennium

Title: Forgotten Truths
1. Bible study 2. Bible criticism, interpretation 3. Eschatology

ISBN: 978-108-819-710-3

Trumpet Press is a member of the *Christian Indie Publisher's Association* (CIPA).

Two Books

Publisher's Preface 4

Book 1:

UNFULFILLED PROPHECY And The Hope of The Church

Table of Contents 5

Book 2:

FORGOTTEN TRUTHS

Table of Contents 6

Book 1:

UNFULFILLED PROPHECY And The Hope of The Church 7

Book 2:

FORGOTTEN TRUTHS 56

Publisher's Preface

Can the Lord come back before the elect are saved? This and many other questions are answered in Sir Robert Anderson's thought-provoking study. He was one of the most popular lay preachers and Christian apologists of his day. He believed that the Bible was the inerrant word of God, and in this popular 1914 work, he corrects some mistaken beliefs about the Word of God that are still held by devoted Christians today. From the special blessing God bestows upon Gentiles to misconceptions about how and when Jesus will return, Anderson sets the facts straight, as he interprets them from the Bible, and in the process inspires a return to a strict reading of Scripture as the path to true communion with God.

SIR ROBERT ANDERSON (1841-1918) described himself as an anglicized Irishman of Scottish descent. He was raised in a devout Christian home, and led a religious life with occasional transient bouts of penitence and anxiety, until his true conversion at 19, and almost immediately began to preach in Dublin where he trained for a legal profession at Trinity College. A criminal investigator, in 1888 he joined Scotland Yard, London, as Chief of the Criminal Investigation Department, until retirement in 1896. He investigated the Jack the Ripper murders, but he is best remembered for his Bible study books, including *The Coming Prince*, and several others that are still in print today. No doubt, his knowledge as an investigator helped him to analyze the Scriptures.

He was close to some of the greatest biblical teachers of his day, such as James M. Gray, Cyrus Ingersoll Scofield, A. C. Dixon, and E. W. Bullinger. He also preached with John Nelson Darby in Ireland. Anderson was a member of the Plymouth Brethren, first with Darby then with the Open Brethren party before returning to his Presbyterian roots.

UNFULFILLED PROPHECY
And The Hope of The Church

Table of Contents

Chapter 1: 70 Weeks of Daniel 7

Chapter 2: Dating the 70 Weeks of Daniel 10

Chapter 3: 93 Years in the 70 Weeks of Daniel 14

Chapter 4: Has the Church Suplanted Israel? 18

Chapter 5: The Abomination of Desolation.. 24

Chapter 6: The Antichrist, Beast, The Prince, The Man of Sin 29

Chapter 7: The Satanic Influence in the Antichrist 34

Chapter 8: Demonic Influences 39

Chapter 9: Predicting the Future 45

Chapter 10: Three Future Comings of Christ 51

(The Second Edition of this book did not include the short appendix.)

Forgotten Truths

Table of Contents

PREFACE TO THE SECOND EDITION 57

CHAPTER 1: SOME QUESTIONS RAISED 60

CHAPTER 2: ETERNAL WORD OF GOD 62

CHAPTER 3: BLESSING FOR GENTILES 68

CHAPTER 4: GRACE ENTHRONED 77

CHAPTER 5: THE MYSTERY OF CHRIST 82

CHAPTER 6: THE LORD JESUS' RETURN 89

CHAPTER 7: THE GENTILE CHURCH 97

CHAPTER 8: THE SECOND COMING, WHEN? 109

CHAPTER 9: MEANTIME, THE CHURCH AGE 117

CHAPTER 10: WHY THE DELAY 130

CHAPTER 11: "BEMA" OF CHRIST 136

CHAPTER 12: EVANGELIZATION OF THE WORLD 142

(The Appendixes were NOTES on some chapters, and were placed at the end of those chapters.)

UNFULFILLED PROPHECY

CHAPTER 1

70 Weeks of Daniel

Many years ago one of the leading Rabbis of the London Synagogue published a volume of sermons to refute the Christian interpretation of certain Messianic prophecies. The Seventy Weeks of Daniel received prominent notice; and he accused Christian expositors of tampering, not only with chronology, but with the language of Scripture, in their effort to make it apply to the Nazarene. My indignation at such a charge led me to enter upon an extensive course of reading to enable me to refute it. But to my great surprise and distress I found that it was by no means a base-less libel. And this again led me to take up the study of Daniel 9 with an open mind, and a settled determination to accept the words of the prophecy at their face value, and to adopt the standard chronology of the eras and events involved in the inquiry. The error of the received view, that the Captivity era was the basis of the prophecy, was one of my earliest discoveries. And this blunder, trifling though it may seem, has afforded both Jews and Infidels a vantage ground in their attacks upon these Scriptures. There was no "seventy years' Captivity." Because of national sin a judgment of seventy years servitude to Babylon was divinely imposed upon Judah. This judgment fell in the third year of King Jehoiakim (B.C. 606), when Nebuchadnezzar invaded Judea and captured Jerusalem. But his purpose was merely to hold the land as a vassal State, and he left the Jews in undisturbed possession of their City, Daniel and his companions being carried to Babylon to adorn his court as vassal princes.

After three years Jehoiakim revolted; and five years later Nebuchadnezzar returned to enforce his conquest (B.C. 598). And the youthful King Jehoiachin surrendered almost without a struggle. On his first invasion the King of Babylon had proved magnanimous and lenient. But now he had to punish rebellion; and he "carried away all Jerusalem," leaving none behind "save the poorest sort of the people of the land. This was what, in the opening words of his book, Ezekiel terms "King Jehoiachin's captivity," the prophet himself being numbered among the captives.

Jehoiachin's uncle, Zedekiah, was placed upon the throne as vassal king, having sworn allegiance to his suzerain. In common with "the residue of Jerusalem that remained in the land," he had ever before him Jeremiah's warnings that a refusal to submit to the Divine decree which brought them under servitude to Babylon would bring upon them a far more terrible judgment. Nebuchadnezzar would again return to "destroy them utterly," and to make the land "a desolation and an astonishment." But they gave heed to false prophets who pandered to the national vanity by predicting a speedy restoration of their independence; and having obtained a promise of armed support from Egypt, the Jews again revolted.

Nebuchadnezzar thereupon invaded Judea for the third time; and when, after a siege of eighteen months, he captured Jerusalem, the city was given up to fire and sword. The last chapter of 2 Chronicles contains the sad story of Judah's sin and of the Divine judgments it brought upon them.

Three several judgments, distinct, though in part concurrent, thus befell that stiff-necked people. And it was this third judgment of the "Desolations" that filled the thoughts and bowed the heart of Daniel, as he prayed the prayer which brought him the great prophecy of the Seventy Weeks. No words could be plainer or more definite. "I Daniel understood by the books the number of the years whereof the word of the Lord came to Jeremiah the prophet, for the accomplishing of the Desolations of Jerusalem, even seventy years." And by those same "books" he would have understood also that the seventy years of the "Servitude" were on the point of expiring. And, of course, the return of the exiles would bring to an end the judgment of the "Captivity," which thus lasted sixty-two years.

But as Daniel had already passed his fourscore years of life he would scarcely hope to outlive the Desolations, seventeen years of which had still to run. And I confidently offer the suggestion that his prayer was an appeal that God would cancel those years, and remit the still unexpired portion of the judgment. The circumstances of the time, and the whole tenor of the prayer, seem to point to this. The closing words are specially explicit: "O Lord forgive; O Lord hearken and do; defer not, for Thine own sake, O my God; for Thy city and Thy people are called by Thy name." What more there was in his heart to utter we know not; for "while he was speaking in prayer" the angel Gabriel appeared to him - the same heavenly messenger who heralded in later times the Savior's birth in which should be read as in Bethlehem, and from him the prophet received, in answer to his supplication, the great prophecy of the Seventy Weeks.

Here are the words: "Seventy weeks are decreed upon thy people and upon thy holy city, to finish transgression, and to make an end of sins, and to make reconciliation for iniquity, and to bring in everlasting righteousness, and to seal up vision and prophecy, and to anoint the most holy. Know therefore and discern, that from the going forth of the commandment to restore and to build Jerusalem, unto the Messiah the Prince, shall be seven weeks, and threescore and two weeks: it shall be built again, with street and moat, even in troublous times. And after the threescore and two weeks shall Messiah be cut off, and shall have nothing: and the people of the Prince that shall come shall destroy the city and the sanctuary; and the end thereof shall be with a flood, and even unto the end shall be war; desolations are determined. And he shall make a firm covenant with many for one week; and for the half of the week he shall cause the sacrifice and the oblation to cease, and upon the wing of abominations shall come one that maketh desolate, even until the consummation, and that determined, shall wrath be poured out upon the desolator."

CHAPTER 2

Dating the 70 Weeks of Daniel

The Hebrew Scriptures contain no Messianic prophecy that is simpler and more definite than this of the Seventy Weeks, and none better fitted to silence the infidel and convince the Jew. But its meaning and evidential value are lost in a bewildering maze of forced or fanciful interpretations. And this is the evil work of Christian expositors! The meaning of the language of the prophecy may be deemed matter for discussion; but no intelligent reader, whether he be Christian or Jew or Infidel, who will study it with an unbiased mind, can entertain an honest doubt as to what it says. Echoing the words of Daniel's prayer, the angel's message told him that not seventy years, but seventy weeks of years were decreed upon his people and his holy city, before they would enter into full Divine blessing.

This era is divided into three portions, of seven weeks, sixty-two weeks, and one week, respectively. It dates from the issuing of a decree to build Jerusalem. From that event "unto Messiah the prince" there were to be 7+ 62 weeks. And after "the sixty-two weeks" the Messiah would be "cut off." The seventieth and last week of the era would be signalized by the advent of another Prince, who would make a seven years' covenant (or treaty) with the Jews; and in the middle of the week (i.e., after three years and a half), he would violate that treaty and suppress their Temple worship and the ordinances of their religion.

All this is so plain that any intelligent child could understand it.

We must remember, however, that with the Jews in ancient times it was as natural to speak of a week of years as of a week of days. And further, that their year was one of three hundred and sixty days. Such was the year in use in Babylon, where the prophecy was given. And, moreover, it was the year by which the judgment of the "Desolations" to which the prophecy referred, was reckoned. That era dated from the day on which the city was invested; namely, the 10th Tebeth in the ninth year of Zedekiah -a day that for four and twenty centuries has been observed as a fast by the Jews in every land. And, as the Prophecy of Haggai so explicitly records, it ended on the twenty-fourth day of Chisleu in the second year of Darius Hystaspes.

Now from the 10th Tebeth B.C. 589 to the 24th Chisleu, B.C. 520, was a period of 25,200 days, or seventy years of 360 days.

The first question then which claims attention relates to the "decree" to rebuild the city. And at this point most expositors proceed to discuss various recorded edicts for the return of the exiles, or for building or adorning the Temple. But if we refuse to treat Divine prophecy in the loose and careless way we read a newspaper or a novel, we shall seize upon the fact that Jerusalem was rebuilt in pursuance of an edict issued by King Artaxerxes of Persia in the twentieth year of his reign; and that history, sacred and profane, knows nothing of any other "decree" for the rebuilding of the holy city.

Nehemiah was cupbearer to the King-"an office of high honor in Persia," and his Book opens by mentioning that certain Jews arrived at the Persian capital bringing him grievous tidings of the condition of Jerusalem. The second chapter narrates that, while discharging the duties of his office, the King taxed him with showing signs of private grief in the royal presence. "Why should not my countenance be sad?" he pleaded, "when the city, the place of my fathers' sepulchres, lieth waste, and the gates thereof are burned with fire?" "For what dost thou make request?" the King demanded; and Nehemiah answered, "That thou wouldest send me to Judah, unto the city of my father's sepulchres, that I may build it." The King thereupon authorized Nehemiah to undertake the work of restoration; and before the next Feast of Tabernacles Jerusalem was again a walled city, secured by gates and ramparts.

Our next enquiry is whether sixty-nine weeks of years, measured from the date of that edict, ended with any event to satisfy the words, "unto Messiah the Prince." And here we must remember that the Cross, and not the Incarnation, was the world's great "crisis." And while Scripture nowhere records the Savior's birth date, the epoch of His ministry is given, with absolute definiteness, as occurring in the fifteenth year of Tiberius Caesar. Now (pace the "reconcilers" and expositors) "the reign of Tiberius, as beginning from the 19th Augustus A.D. 14, was as well-known a date in the time of Luke as is the reign of Queen Victoria in our own day; and no single case has ever been produced in which his regnal years were reckoned in any other manner." We can thus definitely fix upon Nisan A.D. 29 as the date of the first Passover of our Lord's ministry.

And as His ministry ex-tended over four Passovers, it is as certain as inspired Scripture and human language can make it that the date of the Crucifixion was the Festival of Nisan, A.D. 32.

In accordance with Jewish custom, the Lord went up to Jerusalem "six days before the Passover," i.e., on Friday, the 8th Nisan. Presumably He spent the Sabbath in Bethany; and in the evening, when the Sabbath was ended, there took place the supper in Martha's house. And upon the following day, the 10th Nisan, He made His "triumphal entry" into Jerusalem. No careful student of the narrative can fail to recognize that this was, both in intention and in fact, a crisis in His ministry. After the great Council of the nation had decreed His death He charged His Apostles not to make Him known; and from that time He shunned all public recognition of His Messiahship. But now He welcomed the acclamations of "the whole multitude of the disciples," and silenced the remonstrances of the Pharisees by declaring that "if these held their peace the stones would immediately cry out." For on that day was fulfilled Zechariah's prophecy: "Rejoice greatly, O daughter of Zion! Shout, O daughter of Jerusalem! Behold thy King cometh unto thee, lowly and riding upon an ass." And when the disciples raised the triumphant shout, "Hosanna to the son of David! Blessed is the King of Israel that cometh in the name of the Lord," the Savior looked off toward the Holy City, and exclaimed, "If thou also hadst known even on this day, the things that belong to thy peace! but now they are hid from thine eyes!" "Even on this day," for it was the fateful day on which the sixty-nine weeks of the Daniel prophecy expired. And it was the only occasion in all His earthly sojourn on which He was acclaimed as Messiah the Prince, the King of Israel.

There is no vagueness in Divine reckoning. As the Jewish year was regulated by the Paschal moon, we can calculate the Julian date of any Nisan. The 1st Nisan in the twentieth year of Artaxerxes, when the decree to restore and build Jerusalem was issued, was the 14th March, B.C. 445. And the era intervening between that day and the 10th Nisan (or 6th April), A.D. 32, was 173,880 days, or sixty-nine weeks of years, to the very day. (See Ch. 10 of *The Coming Prince*.) The Artaxerxes date was calculated for me by the Astronomer Royal; and the dates of the years of the Ministry will be found in various standard works upon the subject.

The scheme here unfolded was foreshadowed by Julius Africanus in his Chronography: the detailed elucidation of it is a part of my personal contribution to the interpretation of Daniel. And the result may well give food for thought both to the Christian and the Critic. The skeptical crusade of the Higher Criticism claims to have discredited the Book of Daniel as being either a pseud-epigraph or a romance.

But how then can it account for the fulfillment of this particular prophecy? If someone announced that the distance, say, from the main door of St. Paul's Cathedral to some well-known rural landmark, was exactly 173,880 yards, and the statement was found to be absolutely accurate, what estimate should we form of anyone who dismissed the result as being a mere coincidence or a happy guess? Should we not brand him as either knave or fool? And unless we are to allow our respect for Professors and pundits to outweigh our reverence for God and His holy Word, this must be our estimate of those who either champion or accept the "assured results of the Higher Criticism" respecting the prophecy of Daniel.

CHAPTER 3

93 Years in the 70 Weeks of Daniel

No Christian doubts the Messianic fulfillment of the 69 weeks of this prophecy. And if we distinguish between what is doubted and what is doubtful, no less certain is it that the 70th week awaits fulfillment in a future age.

The suggestion that such an era should be thus interrupted in its course may seem strange and untenable, but the intelligent student of Scripture will recognize the principle which this involves. That principle is strikingly exemplified in the era of four hundred and eighty years, reckoned from the Exodus to the Temple (1 Kings 6). According to the historical books, that period was in fact five hundred and seventy-three years; and this is confirmed by the Apostle's words at Pisidian Antioch (Acts 13:18-31). How then can this difference of ninety-three years be explained? Though this problem has perplexed chronologers the solution of it is plain and simple. These ninety-three years are the sum of the servitudes recorded in the book of Judge. During five several periods Israel's national existence as Jehovah's people was in abeyance when, in punishment for their idolatry, He "sold them into the hands of their enemies." They thus became enslaved to the King of Mesopotamia for eight years, to the King of Moab for eighteen years, to the King of Canaan for twenty years, to the Midianites for seven years, and finally to the Philistines for forty years. (The sum of 8+18+20+7+40 is 93. The servitude of Judges 10:7, 9 affected only the tribes beyond Jordan, and did not suspend Israel's national position.) When God forgives our sins He blots out the record of them.

And if this principle obtains even in reckoning an historical era, how legitimate it seems in the case of a prophetical era like that of the Seventy Weeks. By their rejection of Messiah, Israel forfeited their normal position of privilege and special blessing. And seeing that Messianic prophecy runs in the channel of Israel's national history as the covenant people, its fulfillment is tided back until the Loammi sentence which now rests upon them is withdrawn.

The 24th chapter of Matthew, moreover, is an end of controversy on the question here at issue. The first book of the New Testament, like the last, is prophetic. And the 24th chapter is well described by Dean Alford as "the anchor of Apocalyptic interpretations." To understand it aright we must shake free from traditional exegesis, and read it with intelligent appreciation of the position and attitude of those to whom it was addressed. They were men whose thoughts were molded and whose hopes were based upon the Hebrew Scriptures. And when they put the question, "What shall be the sign of Thy Coming and of the winding-up of the age?" they had in view the age of Israel's subjection to Gentile supremacy and the Coming again of Christ "to restore the Kingdom to Israel." It is extraordinary that any intelligent reader should confound that event with the Coming revealed in the Epistles. The one is the Coming foretold in Hebrew prophecy, which will bring deliverance to the favored nation in days to come. The Lord here terms it "the coming of the Son of Man," a Messianic title which never occurs in the Epistles, and is never used in Scripture save in relation to His earthly people. But the Coming revealed in the Epistles is one of the "mystery" truths of Christianity; a "Coming" to call up to their heavenly home the redeemed of this Christian dispensation.

These "Comings" have nothing in common save that both refer to the same Christ. With still greater force does this remark apply to "the Second Advent" of theology, an event which will be not less than a thousand years later than "the Coming of the Son of Man." For the Coming foretold in Matthew 24, 25 will inaugurate the kingdom of heaven upon earth-"the millennial reign of Christ" (to use a theological phrase), whereas "the Second Advent" of theology is

His coming to judgment at the end of that thousand years. There can be no intelligent study of unfulfilled prophecy if we fail to distinguish between these several "Comings" of Christ.

Certain it is that if the Coming of Christ of which the Epistles speak be the same as "the Coming of the Son of Man" of Matthew 24, the Apostle's words are in flat and flagrant opposition to the Lord's explicit teaching. For His warning is clear and emphatic that His Coming as Son of Man must not be looked for until after the coming of Antichrist, the horrors of the great Tribulation," and the awful signs and portents foretold in Messianic prophecy. Whereas the Epistles will be searched in vain for even a suggestion that any event of prophecy bars the fulfillment of what Bengel calls "the hope of the Church." If then these several Scriptures relate to the same event, we must jettison either the First Gospel or the Pauline Epistles, for the attempt to reconcile them is hopeless.

But, it may be asked, did not the Lord on that same occasion use the words, "Watch. for ye know not what time your Lord doth come"? Yes, truly; but those words have reference to the waiting time when the Tribulation is past, and all the events foretold to precede His Coming have been fulfilled. For at that juncture the attitude of the earthly people toward the Coming which is their special hope, will be the same as that which is enjoined upon us in this present age -constant expectation of the Lord's return." (Alford.) For, as the Epistle to Titus tells us, the grace-taught Christian learns " to live looking for that blessed Hope." And "looking for" is but a poor equivalent for the Greek word it represents. A still stronger word the Apostle used when, in writing to the Philippians from his Roman prison, he said, "We are looking for the Savior." It is a word that. expresses earnest expectation of something believed to be imminent. According to Bloomfield, "it signifies properly to thrust forward the head and neck, as in anxious expectation of hearing or seeing something." Such was the attitude of the mother of Sisera as she watched for her son's return: Through the window she looked forth, and cried through the lattice, "Why is his chariot so long in coming?" And yet there are religious teachers who assert, and sometimes with dogmatic vehemence, that the Lord cannot come until after the Tribulation, thus relegating the "blessed hope" to the sphere of other Christian hopes which, like that of the resurrection, for example, though divinely "sure and certain," are indefinitely remote. Indeed, this teaching absolutely kills the hope. For we recall the Savior's words that "except those days should be shortened" none of His people would survive them. And this being so, it would surely be our longing wish and prayer that He would let us pass to heaven by death before the advent of such evil times.

Nor is this all. For this question may be viewed from another standpoint. We are Divinely exhorted to live in constant expectation of the Coming of the Lord; to stand with our hand upon the latch, as it were, in readiness to obey His call. And yet, we are assured of a long-drawn-out warning of His coming, not only by the fiercest persecution earth has ever known, but also by a series of appalling signs and portents in the sphere of nature! Suppose that some chapter of a novel should contain the story of a man who announces to his retinue of servants that he is going abroad, and may be absent for a considerable time. The date of his return he cannot fix, but he assures them that they shall have a very clear and ample warning notice of it. And yet, at the same time, he goes on to impress upon them to live in constant expectation of his coming back, for any day and any hour he may walk in upon them. Should we not throw down the book with feelings either of amusement or contempt for such utter nonsense? What, then, shall be our estimate of the teaching above impugned, remembering that on a theme so sacred as that of our Lord's return all folly is profane?" (If the master told his servants that between the warning notice of his coming and his actual arrival there would be an interval, and that during that interval they might expect him any day and any hour, the story would exemplify the difference between the words of verses 4-0 and of verses 33-44 of Matt. 24.)

CHAPTER 4

Has the Church Suplanted Israel?

The fulfillment of the Seventieth week of Daniel clearly pertains to a time that is within the scope of other visions granted to the prophet, and also of other Apocalyptic visions to which these are inseparably allied. At this stage of our inquiry, therefore, we enter a field of heated controversy; and it may be well, before proceeding, to consider the principles which should guide our further progress.

And this inquiry will be facilitated by a brief survey of the scheme of Divine prophecy as a whole.

Until comparatively recent years the majority of prophetic students were ranged in one or other of the rival camps of futurist or historicist interpretation. But in these more enlightened days most of us have come to recognize the truth of Bacon's words, that "Divine prophecies, being of the nature of their Author, with whom a thousand years are but as one day, and, therefore, are not fulfilled punctually at once, but have springing and germinant accomplishment throughout many ages though the height or fullness of them may refer to some one age." We refuse to believe, therefore as the futurist system would imply, that Messianic prophecy has no voice for this age of Israel's rejection. And no one who understands aright what may be termed the ground plan of the Bible will enlist in the camp of the historicists. For that system, as formulated by its accredited exponents, displays utter ignorance respecting the place which Israel holds in the Divinely-revealed purposes for earth, and also as to the peculiar character of this Christian dispensation and the distinctive truths pertaining to it.

In its spiritual aspect the Bible is the story of redemption; and we know from the Lord's own teaching that it speaks of Him in every part of it. In the record of His post-resurrection ministry we read that "the Lord expounded in all the Scriptures the things concerning Himself." (This threefold division of the sacred Canon was familiar to every Hebrew. The Psalms being the first book of the third division, gave its name to it.)And more definite still are His words to the disciples on the day of the Ascension, "that all things must be fulfilled which were written in the law of Moses, and in the prophets and in the Psalms concerning Me."

But the Bible has also an exoteric aspect. And when thus read, what do we find? A brief preface tells of the Creation and the Fall; of the judgment of the Flood; of the apostasy of the Noachian age; and of the building of Babel, and its consequences. The events of more than twenty centuries are thus dismissed in the eleven chapters that lead up to the call of Abraham. And the rest of the Old Testament relates to the Abrahamic race; the great Gentile nations of antiquity coming under notice only in connection with Israel. For Israel was chosen of God to be His witnesses and agents upon earth. As the Apostle to the Gentiles wrote to a Gentile church, "to them (Israel) were committed the oracles of God;" and of them, "as concerning the flesh, Christ came." And with emphasis he wrote also, "God hath not cast away His people whom He foreknew"; and the receiving of them again to favor will be as life from the dead " in blessing to the world.

But ever since the days of the Latin Fathers Christendom religion has been obsessed by the error of supposing that "the Church" has supplanted Israel in the Divine scheme of prophecy; that God has jettisoned His revealed purposes for earth in relation to the Covenant people; and that when "the number of His elect" of this dispensation is complete, earth and its inhabitants will be engulfed in a cataclysm of judgment fire. But human sin cannot thwart the purposes of God, albeit the realization of them may thus be delayed. And no Divine word of prophecy or promise can ever fail. The prophecy of Israel's sacred calendar, for example, shall be fulfilled in every part of it. For even the festivals which marked the successive stages of the annual harvest of the land are a veiled prophecy of the harvest of redemption.

The sheaf of the first fruits at Passover speaks of Christ and His resurrection from the dead. The "two wave loaves" of Pentecost point forward to the two houses of Israel in full acceptance with God in days to come. And when, at the Feast of Tabernacles, the Israelites assembled in Jerusalem with palm branches in their hands, the celebration typified the harvest-home of redemption - earth's great "Feast of Ingathering," when the palm-bearing host of the redeemed of an age still future, an innumerable multitude "out of all nations and kindreds and peoples and tongues," shall raise their loud-voiced cry of praise to God.

The popular conception of the Divine "plan of the ages" may be epigrammatically described as a pandemonium ending with a conflagration. How vastly different is it from the scheme revealed in Scripture? For all Hebrew prophecy, from Moses to Malachi, speaks of "times of restitution of all things, or, in other words, of a coming age when everything shall be put right on earth by a reign of righteousness and peace.

And this was the burden of the Baptist's preaching, and of the early ministry of the Lord and His Apostles. "The kingdom of heaven is at hand" was not "the gospel" as we understand the word; it heralded the advent of the promised "times of restitution," when the heavens shall rule upon the earth.

But though Israel's Messiah-King was in their midst "His own received Him not," and His death on Calvary was the response the nation made to that "gospel of the kingdom." His intercessory prayer upon the cross obtained for them a respite from the consequences of that awful sin; and at Pentecost the Apostle of the Circumcision was inspired to proclaim that a national repentance would bring back "the Christ who before was preached unto them," and usher in the promised age of blessing. But Israel was obdurate, and the murder of Stephen was the answer made to the Pentecostal amnesty. He was the messenger sent after the King to say they would not have

Him to reign over them. So "there was no remedy," and instead of sending back the Christ, God sent them the awful judgment under which the nation still lies prostrate. After the death of Stephen, the Apostle Paul received his call. It is generally over-looked that, though his commission was specially to the Gentiles, it included a definite mission to Israel And in fulfillment of that mission he traversed all Jewry, from Jerusalem round to Rome. And in every place his first appeal was to the Synagogue.

But though individual Jews responded to the Gospel, not a single synagogue accepted the proffered mercy. That part of his commission, therefore, was fulfilled, when "the chief of the Jews" in Rome rejected his testimony; and the Book of the Acts closes by proclaiming that "the salvation of God was sent unto the Gentiles." And surely the fact is significant that it is in "the Captivity Epistles," written after that crisis in his ministry, that we find the full revelation of the distinctive truths of Christianity.

Then as to principles of interpretation; if at a meeting of the Great Sanhedrin in Jerusalem, two thousand years ago, some learned Rabbi had ventured to offer a strictly Scriptural forecast of the coming and career of Christ, he would doubtless have been silenced by the indignant rebuke that such literalness of exegesis was fitted to bring discredit upon Holy Scripture. And yet we now read those very prophecies with knowledge of their fulfillment even in minute details.

Here are a few of them:

"A virgin shall conceive and bear a son";
"thy King cometh unto thee . . . riding upon an ass";
"they weighed for my price thirty pieces of silver";
"and I took the thirty pieces of silver and cast them to the potter in the house of the Lord";
"they part my garments among them and cast lots upon my vesture";
"they pierced my hands and my feet";
"they gave me vinegar to drink."

To the prophets themselves such words were full of mystery; and no doubt they were generally "explained away" as mere poetry. And yet in every jot and tittle of them they found their counterpart in fact. Seeing then that the Scriptural records of such fulfillments are our best, if not our only, guide in dealing with prophecies that were still unfulfilled at the close of the sacred Canon, we may unreservedly accept the principle of literal fulfillment in our study of them.

We shall therefore take careful note of the prefatory words of Gabriel's prophecy, echoing the concluding words of Daniel's prayer: "Seventy weeks are decreed upon thy people and thy holy city." And we shall reject any scheme of interpretation that finds the fulfillment of this prophecy in the present dispensation when Jerusalem is a Gentile city, and Israel is Lo-ammi.

But while insisting on the principle of literal fulfillment, we must not reject the other principle of "germinant accomplishment." For Scripture itself affords some striking illustrations of it; as, for example, the Lord's reference to the Baptist as being the Elijah of Malachi's prophecy. "If ye are willing to receive him (He said) this is Elijah." And yet at a later date he said, "Elijah truly shall first come and restore all things." And especially apt is the Apostle Peter's reference to the outpouring of the Spirit at Pentecost as being within the scope of Joel's prophecy -the fulfillment of which pertains to an age after Israel has been restored to national prosperity and spiritual blessing. For this is the burden of Joel's prophecy. In the present age of Israel's rejection, Jew and Gentile stand by nature upon the same level of guilt and doom. "There is no difference, for all have sinned." But neither is there any difference as regards salvation. Grace is reigning, and therefore "there is no difference, for the same Lord is rich unto all that call upon Him."

The Jew shall have blessing as freely as his neighbor, if only he will give up his boasted vantage ground of covenant and promise. Blessing on that ground is as inconsistent with grace, as is blessing on the ground of works, or of personal merit of any kind. For in the same sense in which we say that "God cannot lie," we recognize that He cannot act upon incompatible principles at the same time.

It is clear, therefore, that before this prophecy of the Seventy Weeks can be fulfilled for Daniel's people, there must be a change of dispensation as definite and vital as that which took place when Israel was rejected and set aside. Israel's outcast condition is one of the "mystery" truths of this Christian dispensation. (It was in grace that God gave the covenant; but the covenant established a relationship; and, for those who were within it, blessing was on that ground. But when the Cross put an end to every claim upon God, the only alternatives were grace or judgment.) But this dispensation will be brought to an end when the Lord rises up from the throne of grace and, in fulfillment of that other "mystery," comes for His heavenly people, including both Jews and Gentiles, who are one with himself as members of "the Church which is his body." And then the earthly people will come to their own again; and "the receiving of them" will be fraught with widespread blessing.

The prophecy of Zechariah points forward to "that day" when there will be a great national and spiritual revival among them in their own city and land. And the blessings promised to them in Daniel 9:24 await "that day" of Zechariah 13:1. In no part of them have these blessings yet been realized for Israel.

CHAPTER 5

The Abomination of Desolation

The Lord's reference to "the abomination of desolation spoken of by Daniel the prophet," gives the clue to the right interpretation of the unfulfilled portion of the prophecy of the Seventy Weeks. If the Sermon on the Mount is commonly misread. no less so is this " Second Sermon on the Mount," in which that reference occurs. (Matthew 24:15.) To understand it aright we must remember that it is a prophecy; and, as already suggested, we must put ourselves in the place of those to whom it was addressed, and study it as though the present "mystery" dispensation had never intervened, and the predicted events had run their course during the lifetime of the Apostles.

His words were in reply to their inquiry, of verse 3; "What shall be the sign of Thy coming, and of the winding up of the age" And, of course, the" Coming" to which they refer is that of Messianic prophecy, and the "age" is that of Gentile supremacy, which is to last until that Coming. In verse 3 He speaks of the sunteleia of the age; and in verse 14 of its telos (or end). And then, as is so usual in the prophetic Scriptures, He goes back upon the period already covered in brief outline; and in verse 15 He gives them the sign by which they will know that the warned-against terrors of the Great Tribulation are about to break upon them. (v. 21.) Although the events of the siege and capture of Jerusalem by Titus may well be within the scope of the Lord's words, surely no one who studies them in connection with Daniel's prophecy, which the Lord expressly cites, and the other Scriptures relating to the same era, can entertain a doubt that their fulfillment awaits the future restoration of the Covenant People to their own land and to Divine favor.

For the words which the Lord spoke that day upon the Mount of Olives were not "spent (to use a legal term) when the Jewish disciples to whom they were addressed became, so to speak, "denationalized" by being raised to the heavenly relationship of the Body of Christ, in which "there is neither Jew nor Gentile." Like all the words He spoke on earth, they are eternal; and in an age to come they will be read and pondered by an "elect remnant "of Israel, gathered in their own land. We are always keen to mark how clearly the Lord had us in view in much of His teaching; but Christians seem never to realize that, in a passage such as this, He was thinking of His saints in the coming days of the fiercest trial which His people have ever known. If even in this time of their impenitence and rejection "they are beloved for the fathers' sakes," how deep and solicitous must be that love, in view of the coming age of their repentance and faith! Can we doubt that, when the Lord gave utterance to this forecast, His Divine omniscience had in view His Jerusalem saints of that future age in which it will be all fulfilled? Nor can we doubt that, as they scan the newspapers, and watch the gathering clouds of the storm that is about to break upon them, it will be with mind and heart intent upon these sacred words of warning.

And thus they will await the dreaded signal for immediate flight-- "the abomination of desolation, spoken of by Daniel the prophet, standing in the holy place." "History repeats itself." The first holder of the Imperial scepter of Gentile supremacy demanded divine worship for a statue of himself. And the last great Kaiser of the evil line will set up his image, to be worshipped by all, under penalty of death for refusing to render it divine homage. And the language of Daniel 9. 27 is explicit that it will be "upon the Temple" not inside the shrine where none but the priests would see it, but in some prominent position, *coram populo*. And as Satan will be the instigator of this, surely the suggestion is neither wild nor fanciful that the site on which the statue of the Antichrist shall be erected may be "a pinnacle of the Temple," corresponding to that on which the Lord Jesus stood when tempted of the Devil.

The "text-card system" of prophetic study has tended to discredit the Bible. And a knowledge of "dispensational truth" is a safeguard against this influence. For it teaches us, as Bacon quaintly phrased it, "to sort every prophecy of Scripture with the event fulfilling the same." And thus it brings to light the hidden harmony of Holy Writ; and prophetic study, instead of being a pastime for mystics, becomes a confirmation of our faith. As already noticed, "the doctrine of the second advent" is a by-product of this text-card system of exegesis. Every passage that speaks of the Lord's coming again is separated from its context; and all are thrown together, as though they referred to the same event, and are to be fulfilled at the same epoch.

What concerns us here, however, is the prophecy of the Seventy Weeks; and at the cost of some repetition a restatement of the problem may be opportune. That era has to do with Daniel's city and people. The 69th week ended with "the cutting off" of Messiah. Israel was then set aside, and the course of the era was interrupted. And the unfulfilled 70th week will not begin to run until the covenant people are again Divinely recognized. And, as already noticed, that recognition implies a. thorough "change of dispensation." The reign of grace must end. and the members of the heavenly election of this age must be called away from earth before the earthly people can be restored to their own again. (See page 84 *ante*.)

The epoch of the whole era was "the issuing of a decree to restore and build Jerusalem." And the epoch of the final week of the era will be the signing of a treaty by the last great Kaiser- the coming Prince of Daniel 9:27-guaranteeing to the Jews their national rights, with special reference, apparently, to the observance of their national religion. And in the middle of the week he will violate that treaty by the desecration of the Temple; an event that will be followed immediately by "the Great Tribulation." The duration of that persecution is definitely specified as three and a half years, forty-two months, or twelve hundred and sixty days. And it will be brought to a sudden end by the terrible convulsions in the sphere of nature which are to herald the day of wrath.

The Lord's words recorded in Matthew 24:6, ff., have their precise counterpart in the apocalyptic visions of the seals (Rev. 6). His first warning note is of "wars and rumors of wars"; and when the first seal is opened, a white-horsed rider goes forth "conquering and to conquer." The Lord next indicates wars of a more terrible character; and this has its parallel in the appearance of the red-horsed rider of the second seal, to whom is given "a great sword" and "power to take peace from the earth, and that they should kill one another." The wars of the first seal are apparently of the type to which we are accustomed; but those of the second seal will be an orgy of ruthless slaughter. It is not a mere repetition of the preceding vision.

The Lord's next word is "famines"; and when the third seal is broken, the black-horsed rider appears with a pair of balances in his hand, to weigh out the necessaries of life at famine prices. As famines are natural sequence to wars of the type here indicated, no less certainly does pestilence follow famine.

And "pestilence" is the word the Lord next utters; so the rider in the vision of the fourth seal is empowered to kill with "death" -- word that needs no interpreting to any who realize the horrors of epidemic plague. But the judgments of the seals are cumulative, and this rider, whose name is Death, "kills with the sword and with hunger and with pestilence." No rider appears when the fifth seal is broken; but neither the meaning of the vision, nor its place in the scheme of prophecy, is open to doubt. In Matt. 24:8, the Lord describes the judgments of the first four seals as "time beginning of sorrows"; and in verse 9 we read "then shall they deliver you up unto tribulation, and shall kill you; and ye shall be hated of all the nations for My name's sake." The Lord's words in verse 21 teach explicitly that this is the Tribulation, the "time of trouble" of Daniel 12:1; and in the vision of the fifth seal are seen under the altar the souls of the martyred victims of that awful persecution. No less certain is the identity of the events of the sixth seal with those portrayed by the Lord in verse 29. All the events of the preceding seals are such as men can account for on natural principles. But now, in view of the unparalleled sufferings of His people in the great Tribulation, and in response to the prayers of the martyrs of that awful time (Rev. 6:9, 10), God at last puts forth His power; appalling portents in the sphere of nature strike terror into the hearts of the impenitent of every class, from kings to bond-men, and in a universal panic they seek to hide from the coming wrath.

The Lord's words in verse 29 are explicit that the terrors of the sixth seal follow immediately after the Tribulation; and, as the period of the Tribulation is the latter half of the 70th week of Daniel, the events of these seals fall within the chronology of prophecy. But it is a common error to suppose that the events foretold in verses 30 and 31 will immediately follow the close of the 70th week. The vision of the seventh seal is yet to be fulfilled. The *theu* (toto) of verse 30 does not refer to the *telos* of the age, but to its *sunteleia*- not to a definite point in time, but to the whole period here in view-a sense which the word bears in three other verses in this same chapter. And the Lord's teaching in the passage beginning with verse 32 deals with that very period.

And here another parallelism with the vision of the seals suggests itself. In Rom. 8:1, we read: "When he had opened the seventh seal there was silence in heaven about the space of half-an-hour." May not this mysterious lull symbolize the very period here in view? What its duration will be we know not, save that it will be within the life-time of that generation, and yet that it will be sufficiently prolonged to make the world forget the preceding terrors, and to make His people need exhortations to sustained watchfulness. "As in the days that were before the flood they were eating and drinking, marrying and giving in marriage," so will it be then. Signs and portents in abundance mark the *sunteleta* of that age, but its *telos* will be unheralded and sudden. In answer to His disciples' question, I again repeat, He warned them to watch, not for His coming, but for the events which must precede it. But now that these events are all fulfilled, his word is "Watch, for ye know not what hour your Lord doth come." For time day and hour of the coming of the Son of Man is a secret unrevealed.

CHAPTER 6

The Antichrist, Beast, The Prince, The Man of Sin

"The people of the Prince who is coming will destroy the city and the sanctuary" (Daniel 9. 26).

Who is this Prince? The manner in which he is here mentioned enables us to answer this question with confidence. For it is not by way of a new revelation, but of incidental reference to sonic one of whose personality and coming Daniel was already aware. There can be no doubt, therefore, that he is "the King of fierce countenance" of the vision accorded to the prophet two years before. And it is universally recognized that the Antichrist of Hebrew prophecy is identical with the Antichrist of the New Testament.

The view that time Coming Prince is the Messiah might be ignored, were it, not that some eminent names can be cited in support of it. Indeed, it is sufficiently refuted by time fact that it is by the people of this Prince that the city and sanctuary will be destroyed. To find the fulfillment of this in the action of the Zealots during the Titus siege indicates to what lengths some expositors will go in support of a false system of exegesis. For the suggestion that Holy Scripture would describe religious apostates as the Lord's people savors of profanity.

A like remark applies to that wild vagary of exegesis that the Lord made a seven years' covenant with the Jewish people, and brought it to an end by His death "in the midst of the week." And the figment that His death put an end to "sacrifice and oblation" savors of the ignorance of apostate Christendom.

The Jew is more intelligent in this respect than the nominal Christian; for he knows that, until this sin-defiled earth has been purified by fire, there can be neither altar nor shrine without "sacrifice and oblation." And when, in the future age of the kingdom, a regenerate Israel will assemble in their divinely-ordered Temple at Jerusalem, the Book of Ezekiel will give them in full detail the Divinely revised ritual to guide their worship.

> * (They will doubtless note what that ritual is and what it retains of the Mosaic cult. They will read Ezekiel with the Epistle to the Hebrews in their hands; and they will not fail to distinguish between sin offerings in relation to ceremonial uncleanness, and the great sin-offering which typified what the death of Christ accomplished in putting away the sins of the people. In that aspect of it the sin-offering can never be repeated. As the Epistle to the Hebrews teaches, the Christian place of worship is the sanctuary above, with its heavenly altar and Great High Priest. On this subject I would refer to Bishop Lightfoot's *Commentary on Philippians*, pp. 181-185.)

The word "Antichrist" occurs nowhere in Scripture save in the Epistles of John. But it is recognized that the title applies to the Kaiser of Daniel's visions, to the Man of Sin of 2 Thessalonians, and to the "Beast" of the Apocalypse.

Belief in a personal Antichrist was universal in the Early Church, and it held undisputed sway for more than a thousand years. But when the apostasy of Christendom was fully developed, it was only natural that Christians should raise the question whether the prophecies of Antichrist might not find their fulfillment in Rome. And this belief very generally prevailed until the Evangelical revival of the nineteenth century. In these days of ours Protestantism has no such champions as were the men of that revival. And what led to their change of view was no weakening of their antipathy to Rome but a more intelligent study of Holy Scripture. They awoke to the discovery that this Christian dispensation" denotes neither the failure nor the abandonment of the Divine "plan of the ages." They came to understand the place which the earthly people of the covenant hold in that plan, and to realize that although both the Abrahamic and the Davidic covenants are now in abeyance, they have not been cancelled; and that when this dispensation is brought to an end by the Lord's coming to call His heavenly people home, the main stream of Messianic prophecy will resume its course as though this Christian age had never intervened.

Holy Scripture had long been like an elaborate mosaic, of which the several parts had been disturbed, and the main design for-gotten. But its hidden harmony was brought to light by the study of "dispensational truth" (an apt phrase that was much in use in those days). And that study included the "mystery" truths of this distinctively Christian revelation, truths which had been lost in the interval between the Apostolic age and the era of the great Patristic theologians.

Although traces of these truths may be found in the writings of the Fathers, they have no place in their "systematic theology." They confounded the true Church, the Body of Christ, with the Professing Church on earth -- a departure from the faith which is the root error of the Roman apostasy. And they confounded the Lord's coming at the close of this Christian dispensation with His coming for the deliverance of His earthly people in a future age. And they also confounded grace with covenant, and thus let slip the basal truth of Christianity.

For the doctrines which generally pass for Christian truths are older even than the Divinely-ordered religion of Judaism. The truth of the first coming of Christ is as old as the Eden promise of "the woman's seed." And atonement by His death is as old as Abel's sacrifice. His coming again to judgment dates back to the prophecy of "Enoch the seventh from Adam;" and justification by faith was revealed to Abraham. But not until we reach the Epistles of the New Testament do we find the "mystery" truths of Christianity - truths, that is, which had not been revealed in the earlier Scriptures. As, for example, "the mystery of the Gospel" -- the great basal truth of the reign of grace; the "mystery" of the Church, the Body of Christ, with its heavenly calling and hope; and the "mystery" of that coming of the Lord which will bring the present dispensation to a close.

The study of "dispensational truth" in no way undermines the principle of "germinant accomplishment" of the prophecies, which is the element of truth in the "historicist" scheme of interpretation; but it exposes and refutes the pretensions of that scheme to finality of fulfillment. The evil of that system is not merely that it limits and perverts the scope and meaning of special chapters and isolated texts, but that, in doing this, it tends to discredit the Bible altogether. And as Adolf Saphir wrote, it thus prepared the way for the attacks of Rationalism and Neology.

Moreover, this "Protestant interpretation" became an anachronism when the Pope lost his" temporal power," and Rome became the capital of the Italian kingdom. This event led the" historicists "to adopt the view that the Antichrist was not the Pope, but the Church of which he is the head. But Revelation 17 is explicit that "the Harlot" is distinct from "the Beast"; and therefore every proof that the scarlet woman is the Apostate Church is a further proof that she cannot be the Antichrist.

The pretensions of Rome reach their climax in claiming that the Pope is the vicar of Christ, whereas the Kaiser of prophecy will demand universal worship as being himself the Messiah. He is not a Vice Christ, but Antichrist. As the Lord expressly declared, "he will come in his own name." He will be the impersonation of "the mystery of lawlessness," whereas the Pope and the Church of Rome are merely its most advanced exponents and representatives. Every sacerdotalist, everyone who believes in "the Holy Catholic Church," save in the sense in which the Reformers defined it - in a word, everyone who puts "religion" in the place of Christ, and in any way denies that He is the only Mediator between God and man - is an Antichrist in the same sense in which the Pope is Antichrist. The difference is one merely of degree.

A single instance must here suffice to justify my charge against "the continuous historical interpretation" scheme. Elliott's *Horae Apocalyptica*, is the standard text-book of the cult. Its first five chapters may well impress us with a sense of the value of the writer's scheme. But when he passes from the first five seals to explain that the vision of the sixth seal was fulfilled by the downfall of Paganism in the fourth century, we suffer a revulsion of feeling proportionate to our sense of the "trueness" and solemnity of Holy Writ.

For the closing verses of Rev. 6 are a passage the awful solemnity of which has no parallel in Scripture, save in the kindred prophecies of Isaiah and Joel, and of the Lord Himself in Matthew 24.

They speak of the dread dies ire, ending with the words, "the great day of His wrath is come, and who shall be able to stand?" If it be urged that the events of fifteen centuries ago were within the scope of the prophecy we can consider the matter on its merits; but when we are told that the prophecy was thus fulfilled, we can hold no parley with the teaching. It is the merest trifling with Scripture.

Moreover, it clashes with the charter truth of Christianity. For if the day of wrath has come, the day of grace is past, and the gospel of grace is no longer a Divine message to mankind. To suppose that the day of wrath can be an episode in this dispensation of grace betrays ignorance of grace and brings Divine wrath into contempt. The grace of God in this day of grace surpasses human thought, and His wrath in the day of wrath will be no less Divine. The opening of the sixth seal heralds the dawning of that awful day; the visions of the seventh seal unfold its unutterable terrors. But, we are told, the pouring out of the vials, "the seven plagues which are the last, or in them is finished the wrath of God" (Rev. 15:1, R.V.), is being now accomplished. The sinner, therefore, may comfort himself with the knowledge that divine wrath is but stage thunder which, in a practical and busy world, may safely be ignored! Even in Apostolic times there were many Antichrists: in these days of ours they are innumerable.

During the last half-century their influence has undermined the Protestantism of our National Church.

The Evangelicals have become a dwindling minority, and the "Evangelical Party" is but a memory of the past. During the same period a crusade of systematized infidelity has corrupted all the Churches of the Reformation. And side by side with these phases of the apostasy is the rise and spread of demon cults, some of which overawe their votaries by a display of genuine miraculous power.

The times are full of peril, and we need to realize that all these antichristian movements are preparing the way for Antichrist himself.

It is of practical importance, therefore, to note what Scripture teaches respecting his character and career. And this will appear in a further study of the prophecy of the Seventy Weeks.

CHAPTER 7

The Satanic Influence in the Antichrist

The belief of early times, that the Antichrist will be personally energized by Satan, was based on Scripture. For his coming, we are told, will be "after the working of Satan, with all power and signs and lying wonders." Still more explicit is the language of the Apocalyptic vision, that "the Dragon gave him his power and his throne and great authority." And we recall the words of the Lord Himself that, in that awful time, false Christs and false prophets "will show great signs and wonders, insomuch that, if it were possible, they will deceive the very elect." To fritter away the meaning of these statements by referring them to the errors and follies of priestcraft is a profane trifling with the Word of God. Indeed, to put it on a lower ground, it is an insult to the intelligence of every Protestant. For no one whose mind has not been "doped" by "Christendom religion" could be duped by its "blasphemous fables and dangerous deceits." Even among spiritual Christians there are but few who attempt to realize what the condition of the Professing Christian Church will be during the age of which these Scriptures speak. In his commentary on Matthew 12:44, Dean Alford describes in a few pregnant sentences its sad history and present condition. And he adds:

> "What the effect of the Captivity was to the Jews, that of the Reformation has been to Christendom. The first evil spirit has been cast out. But by the growth of hypocrisy, secularity, and rationalism the house has become empty, swept and garnished by the decencies of civilization and discoveries of

secular knowledge, but empty of living and earnest faith. And he must read prophecy but ill, who does not see under all these seeming improvements the preparation for the final development of the Man of Sin, the great re-possession when idolatry and the seven more wicked spirits shall bring the outward frame of so-called Christendom to a fearful end."

If the present condition of the Church is a cause of distress and grief to all true Christians, what will it be when they are called home to heaven at the coming of the Lord, and the restraining influence of the Holy Spirit is no longer felt, as it is felt even in these evil days! It will not be the superstitious only who will be deceived by "the signs and wonders of falsehood." Even the infidel will accept their testimony.

His unbelief today is not so unintelligent as is the quasi faith of many who pose as Christians and Ministers of Christ. Like them, he accounts for the miracles of Scripture by the fact "that the Bible was written by orientals for orientals, and that miracle and myth are congenial to the oriental mind." And he appeals to the absence of miracles during the history of Christendom. "If (he says) I witnessed miracles such as are alleged to have occurred in Bible times, I would renounce my infidelity." This is the mental attitude of multitudes of fair-minded men. And thus they spread a net in which they will become entangled in the coming Antichristian age. And if open infidelity capitulates before its "signs and lying wonders," surely the nominal Christians will flock to its shrines and join in its cult.

But, it will be asked, if the Lord's own people are "caught up" at His coming, and nominal Christians accept the Antichrist, who will be the victims of the persecution? Now, first, it is noteworthy that the Antichrist is primarily the persecutor of the "Covenant people." And though, in the Apocalypse, the Great Tribulation embraces Christendom, in Messianic prophecy it is spoken of only in relation to Israel. And while, in ancient times, idolatry was their national sin, the judgments which that sin brought upon them seem to have made them intolerant of idol worship. Indeed, the idolatry of "Christendom religion "is one element that prejudices the Jew against Christianity. No display of miraculous power would lead him to prostrate himself before an image.

And secondly, the difficulty above stated is one of many that are due to our inveterate habit of confounding plausible inferences from Scripture with what Scripture explicitly teaches. It is commonly assumed, and often asserted with emphasis, that in that coming age there will be no salvation for the sinners of Christendom. For is it not written that "God shall send them strong delusion, that they should believe a lie; that they all might be condemned who believed not the truth, but had pleasure in unrighteousness." But this is merely a special application of the great principle that the acceptance or rejection of Christ fixes the destiny of men. And we may not dare to assert that a just and loving God will hold that every unbeliever is a Christ-rejecter.

Even in our own favored land there are very many "church members" who have never heard "the gospel of the grace of God," but have it dinned into their ears continually that "the sacraments," plus a moral and religious life, will win heaven for them. And what of the multitudes who are never "evangelized" in any way? And is there any Scriptural warrant for asserting that some, even in truly Christian circles, who are now "halting between two opinions," may not find mercy when brought to decision by being left behind at the coming of the Lord? All such will have forfeited the heavenly home and the heavenly glory that are the portion of the redeemed of this present dispensation. But we dare not assert that they can never find salvation, and be enrolled in the book of life; albeit they must needs "enter the kingdom" through torture and death, in a persecution more awful than any recorded in the past.

But a difficulty of another kind claims notice; it is argued that, if the Antichrist be energized by Satan, he must be a monster of wickedness. How then can he command the worship of "all that dwell upon the earth"? This difficulty springs from the prevalent belief in the mythical devil of Christendom. Had such a monster appeared in Eden, Eve would have fled from him in terror. But she was "thoroughly deceived" by the real Satan when he posed as the great philanthropists and proclaimed "the gospel of humanity." The characteristics of that Eden gospel are both simple and charming. "Hath God said!" "Ye shall not surely die." "Ye shall be as gods." First, it casts a doubt upon the plain words of the Divine revelation; secondly, it denies the eternal consequences of sin; and thirdly, it proclaims the elevation of humanity.

In this gospel there is everything to attract the "natural" man, and nothing to repel him. And oven here and now, in Christian Britain, it is preached from numberless quasi Christian pulpits; and thousands, even of real Christians, are in some measure deceived and corrupted by it. Who then can doubt that, when it is accredited by a great display of miraculous power, it will gain universal acceptance. We cannot understand aright the prophecies relating to Antichrist unless we realize that, so far from being a monster of hideous mien and loathsome character, Satan is a being whom man, in his estrangement from God, would admire and emulate.

But did not the Lord Jesus brand him as a liar and a murderer? The words here referred to claim the closest scrutiny. They were addressed to the religious leaders of the Jews, devoutly zealous men who, having witnessed His miracles and weighed us teaching, were now plotting His destruction. To them it was He said, "Ye are of your father the Devil, and the desires of your father it is your will to do. He was a murderer from the beginning, and abode not in the truth, because there is no truth in him. When he speaketh the lie he speaketh of his own; for he is a liar and the father of it. And because I tell you the truth ye believe me not." The gloss that the Lord's sayings were always true, and that the Devil told lies, is deplorably trivial.

The lie is here the antithesis to the truth; and the Devil's being a liar is connected with his being "a murderer from the beginning." The beginning of what? We are here vouchsafed a glimpse into a past eternity, when, to the heavenly host was first made known "the mystery of God, even Christ," namely, that a Firstborn was to be revealed, who was "in all things to have the pre-eminence." The wonderful being whom we know as Satan, and whom the Lord saw "fall from heaven as lightning," aspired to that position; and he rebelled against the Divine purpose, and from that hour he has sought to thwart it. This is fully disclosed in the "Temptation" of our Lord.

Who of us makes any serious effort to realise the meaning of that narrative? Having "led Him up," and given Him that mysterious vision of earthly sovereignty, "the Devil said unto Him, 'To thee will I give all this authority and the glory of them, for it hath been delivered unto me, and to whomsoever I will I give it. If thou, therefore, wilt worship before me it shall all be thine.'" This was no mere outburst of profane folly. It was a bold assertion of a disputed right. Satan claims to be the true Messiah, the true Firstborn and heir of creation; and as. such he claims the worship of mankind.

These apocalyptic visions foretell his greatest, as it will be his final, effort to supplant the Christ of God. And to that end he will give to the Antichrist "his power and his throne and his great authority." Can we then be surprised at the sequel, that "all the world wondered after the Beast? And they worshipped the Dragon (Satan, the old Serpent of Eden) which gave power unto the Beast; and they worshipped the Beast, saying, "Who is like unto the Beast?" But even this is not all. For the Seer "beheld another Beast . . . who exerciseth all the power of the first Beast before him, and causeth the earth and them that dwell therein to worship the first Beast." Thus the mystery of the Godhead will be travestied by this trinity of evil - Satan, the Antichrist, and the "False Prophet." And as already noticed, they will be accredited by signs and wonders that would deceive, if that were possible, the very elect. If we appreciate in any measure the awful significance and solemnity of what these Scriptures teach, we shall no longer be deluded by the almost unbelievable folly of seeking their fulfillment in the history of Christendom. It is not unnatural that an unbeliever should regard these visions as the brilliant daydreams of a pious mystic. But that any spiritual Christian should treat them with such utter levity is no less strange than it is deplorable.

CHAPTER 8

Demonic Influences

No intelligent student of these Scriptures can fail to recognize that, in the age to which they point, there will be spiritual forces in operation such as earth has never experienced in the past, and from which the present age has been singularly free. For, as compared with both past and future, this Christian age is marked by altogether peculiar characteristics.

First, "the grace of God, salvation-bringing to all men, has been manifested," and the Lord Jesus is exalted, not only as Prince, but as Savior. Therefore is it that the Divine throne is now a throne, not of judgment, but of grace. And this again explains the mystery of a silent heaven. For "the kindness and love-toward-man of our Savior God has been manifested." He has spoken His last word of mercy, and when again He breaks the silence it will be in wrath. But until the Lord Jesus passes from the throne of grace to the throne of judgment all direct punitive action against human sin is deferred. Before the dawning of the "day of vengeance" "the acceptable year of the Lord" must run its predestined course.

And secondly, the Holy Spirit is now dwelling upon earth. "The promise of the Father" was not merely that believers in Christ should have the Spirit's guidance and help, for that was the portion of the people of God in every age, but that, when the Lord Jesus returned to heaven, He would send the Holy Spirit to take His place on earth, a promise that was fulfilled at Pentecost. So really is He present with us that the greeting from heaven, with which certain of the Epistles open, is only from "the Father and the Lord Jesus Christ." And during His presence with His people upon earth the powers of hell are definitely restrained. But, when the people of the heavenly election are called from earth to their heavenly home, at the Coming of the Lord, that restraint will cease, "the Man of Sin" will be revealed, and the powers of hell will be permitted to operate in ways and to an extent unprecedented in the past.

Another element which tends to a misreading of these prophecies is a want not only of sympathy, but of acquaintance, with the promises and hopes of Israel. As believers of this dispensation "our citizenship is in heaven," whereas Israel's citizenship is earthly. The true Israelite, therefore, in the coming age will not be looking for the Lord to call him away to heaven, but for "the coming of the Son of Man" to "restore again the kingdom to Israel, "and inaugurate the promised rule of the heavens upon earth. The Lord Jesus was "born King of the Jews." And when He began His Ministry by proclaiming that "the kingdom of Heaven is at hand," that "gospel of the kingdom" did not mean that God was about to rule in heaven, but that, in fulfillment of Messianic prophecy, Divine government was about to be established upon earth.

And this explains the attitude and conduct of the Jewish leaders toward the Lord Jesus. They argued that, if He was indeed the Messiah, He was the promised "Son of David," who would put an end to Gentile supremacy and restore the Davidic covenant, which had been in abeyance ever since the imperial scepter was entrusted to the King of Babylon.

(So deep and widespread is ignorance of all this that those of us who are advanced in years remember when the belief prevailed, even among spiritual men "of light and leading," that the Kingdom of Heaven would be established, as of course, by the preaching of the Gospel. If such a belief has survived the apostasy of the last half-century, surely this hideous world war will avail to quench it. Human nature being what it is, there can be no reign of peace on earth without stern and righteous government.)

The Messiah they were looking for would be a conquering hero, who would deliver them from their enemies and revive the glories of the greatest of their kings. And such the future Antichrist will be; not merely a false Messiah in the religious sense, but a mighty Kaiser. The Apocalyptic visions already quoted clearly indicate that he will be a man of transcendent natural qualities. "All the world wondered after the Beast . . . and they worshipped the Beast, saying, Who is like unto the Beast? Who is able to make war with him?" The mingling of Kaisership with Deity is as old as classic Paganism; and it is not altogether unknown in later times. But it will be no mere theory in the case of the Man of prophecy. A great statesman, an orator (v. 5), and a brilliant general - here is the "superman "whom nations will honor, and armies will follow with enthusiasm. And when we take account of the fact that, added to this, he will be endowed with the superhuman powers of Satan, we can understand the words of Christ, that none but the elect of God will refuse to render him Divine homage. In these visions the word "beast" signifies primarily an empire or kingdom, and then it is used to symbolize an individual. The Beast of Rev. 13 is clearly identical with the fourth Beast of Daniel 7 -- the last great Gentile world power.

But in the Apocalypse it appears at a later stage of its development. Three periods of its history are marked in Daniel. In the first it has ten horns. In the second it has eleven, for a little horn comes up among the ten. In the third it has but eight, for three of the ten have been torn away by the eleventh. Up to this point Daniel's vision represents the beast merely as the fourth kingdom upon earth," but here it turns away to describe the action of "the little horn." And at this epoch it is that Revelation 13 opens. The first three stages of the history of "the fourth kingdom" are past, and another has been developed. It is no longer a confederacy of nations bound together by treaty, but of kings subordinate to a Kaiser whose greatness has won for him the supremacy. And this is the Prince of the prophecy of the Seventy Weeks; the Antichrist of the New Testament; the man whom Satan will single out to administer his awful power on earth in days to come, the man to whom he will give his throne, his power and great authority -- all that the Lord Jesus refused in the days of His humiliation. If Expositors are right in assuming that he is the prominent figure in the several visions of the prophet Daniel there seems to be no doubt that he will come to notice first as the ruler of some petty State within the territorial limits of the ancient Grecian Empire.

He is called "a little horn," a symbol that well suits one who should arise from one of those petty principalities which once abounded in Greece. For "a little horn" indicates what he is, not as a man, but as a monarch. In his origin he will, of course, be merely human; and for a time he will be a patron of religion. But after the terrible crisis in his career, at which he sells himself to Satan, he becomes a relentless persecutor, and he ends by claiming divine honor.

This amazing change takes place at an epoch of supreme import in the course of the future age, namely, the middle of the seventieth week of Daniel. For it is an epoch signalized by the war in heaven between the Archangel and the Dragon; when Satan and his angels will be "cast out into the earth," and the Seer bewails mankind because the Devil is come down into their midst, "having great wrath because he knoweth that he hath but a short time." As the Coming Prince of the prophecy of the Seventy Weeks is identical with the Man of Sin of 2 Thessalonians, that Epistle claims notice here. Both the Epistles to that church indicate that a grievous persecution was then raging in Thessalonica, and the Christians had come to believe that the Tribulation of prophecy had begun, and "the day of the Lord was at hand" – "the great and terrible day of Jehovah." Having regard to the teaching of the First Epistle it may seem strange that such an error could prevail. But, owing to the persecution, the Christians, no doubt, could only meet furtively and in scattered groups; and their leaders being possibly in hiding, their knowledge of that Epistle depended probably on what they remembered of it from hearing it "read in church." Moreover, it would appear from chapter 2:2 and 3:17 that they had received a forged letter, as from the Apostle, cancelling or modifying the teaching of the First Epistle. And the Hebrew converts among them would have knowledge of such Scriptures as, e.g., Isaiah 13, Joel 2, and Malachi 4:5. And, with these in view, they might easily glide into the error which the Second Epistle was designed to correct.

The Apostle's words, "I beseech you on behalf of the Coming of our Lord Jesus Christ" (R.V. margin), show clearly that the error against which he was warning them was destructive of the truth he had taught them. They could not live looking for "that blessed hope" (Titus 2:13) if they were living in view of the awful terrors of the Tribulation and the day of the Lord. For these lines of truth are wholly separate. The one is the line of Messianic prophecy, leading up to the coming of Christ as Son of Man, in a future age, for the deliverance of His earthly people, and for the establishment of His earthly Kingdom. The other is not within the range of Messianic prophecy at all, but points to the fulfillment of the hope of His heavenly people of this Christian dispensation. Following the words above quoted, the Apostle proceeds: "For it (the day of the Lord) will not come except the falling away (the apostasy) come first, and the Man of Sin be revealed, the son of perdition, he that opposeth and exalteth himself against all that is called God or that is worshipped. So that he sitteth in the temple of God, setting himself forth as God." These words claim careful attention. The so-called Protestant interpretation of them finds their fulfillment in the Pope's being carried into St. Peter's at Rome, and seated there somewhat higher than the "tabernacle of the host." If St. Peter's were thus divinely recognized as "the temple of God," those of us who reverence, and seek to obey, His Holy Word would promptly make a qualified submission to Rome, and repair at times to the appointed shrine! This Protestant interpretation thus undermines Protestantism altogether! And this is only a very low ground for rejecting it, for such trilling with and perverting of Scripture is deplorable and evil in the extreme. The Apostle's language points to the same crisis as the Lord's words respecting "the abomination of desolation, spoken of by Daniel the prophet." And it will be fulfilled when the Prince of Daniel 9 violates his treaty with the Jewish people, and desecrates the Holy Temple in Jerusalem. The Antichrist will set up his image upon the Temple, to be worshipped by all (see p. 89 ante.) And (on certain "high days," no doubt) he will personally sit enthroned within the Sanctuary, "setting himself forth as God." This twofold desecration is generally overlooked.

But is it credible that any Jew would acknowledge a Gentile as Messiah? Now first, we have no definite ground for assuming that the Man of prophecy may not be an Israelite. And secondly, are we to assume that "all power and signs and wonders of falsehood" would prove unequal to the task of forging a pedigree, and obtaining the acceptance of it by an apostate people? For the "elect" among them will repudiate him. And the language of Daniel 9:27 is noteworthy; it is with the many that he will make the treaty, implying that a minority of the nation will stand aloof and refuse to be a party to it. And lastly, if to the apostates of Christendom "God will send strong delusion that they should believe the lie," is it strange that the apostates of Judaism should also be thus divinely given over to delusion? And, moreover, we are not dealing here with a human forecast, but with a Divine prophecy.

CHAPTER 9

Predicting the Future

"Prophecy is not given to enable us to prophesy, but as a witness to God when the time (of fulfillment) comes." Even if limits of space allowed of it, my appreciation of these words of Pusey's would prevent my indulging here in any forecasts of the future, beyond what Scripture expressly warrants. Certain extra-Scriptural forecasts have been discredited by the present war. For example, the language of the opening verses of Zechariah 14 were taken to indicate that the future siege and capture of Jerusalem will be the work of half-savage Oriental troops. For, it was argued, Western civilization would not tolerate the excesses hers described. How foolish this appears in view of the atrocities perpetrated by the Germans in this war! But while avoiding flights of fancy as to the means by which, and the manner in which, the events foretold in prophecy will come about, we may well take note of present-day movements and occurrences, which seem to be preparing the way for their fulfillment. For example, appeal may be made to the probable effect of the war on the future of Palestine. If the Turk be driven out, the attempt of any one of the Entente Powers to seize possession of that land would be the signal for another war! And this consideration will, in all probability, lead to its being constituted a protected Jewish State.

And thus the present generation may possibly witness the building of the very temple upon which the Prince of Daniels prophecy will yet set up his image. But this is merely a probable surmise, and the introduction of it here is possibly an indiscretion.

If Pusey's axiom were construed strictly the study of prophecy would be valueless until the time of its fulfillment. But this was far from his intention. For not only is it of fascinating interest to the thoughtful, but of great practical importance to every Christian. It serves to put us on our guard against evil influences and movements, of which the ultimate development and full fruition are described in the prophetic Word. Spiritualism, Christian Science, and other cults of a similar character, may be mentioned in this connection. These cults are daily winning over not a few, even among those whose Christian profession seemed to be above reproach. And the experience of many gives proof that those who yield to these demon influences soon reach a stage where recovery seems impossible, even if they wish to escape from them.

In view of the genuine miracles by which they are accredited, to denounce them as mere charlatanism is idle. And as their miracles are of a beneficent character their votaries regard them as Divine. In dark days of persecution Satan was as "a roaring lion, seeking whom he might devour." And in that character he will be known in the darker period of the coming age. But now "he fashions himself as an angel of light," even as he did in Eden, and in the Temptation of the Lord.

But, it may be asked, how can this be reconciled with what was stated on a preceding page as to the contrast between the present age and that which is to follow it? Here we must be guided by what Scripture records of former "changes of dispensation." These changes find an illustration in the sphere of nature. For while Science can mark with accuracy the changes of the seasons, the actual transition is unnoticed by the observer. And this has its parallel in the spiritual sphere. The law and the prophets were until John, and then the Kingdom of God was preached. But yet the Lord reproached the Jews that though they could discern the face of the sky they could not discern the signs of the tunes. And so was it again when Israel was set aside, and the present Christian dispensation was inaugurated. The change was a crisis of extreme significance, but yet it passed unnoticed; and many characteristics of the new dispensation had marked the later stages of that which it superseded.

And as we observe the present-day manifestations of the sinister spiritualist influences and movements which will be fully developed in the coming age, may we not hail it as giving hope that the present dispensation is nearing its end, and that "the coming of the Lord is drawing nigh?" And that hope will be intensified if we are given to see "the land of the promise" restored to the people of the Covenant.

On yet another ground the practical importance of prophetic study is incalculable. To all who pursue it intelligently it affords full and irrefutable proofs of the Divine authorship of the Bible, and it thus provides an antidote to the poison of the "Higher Criticism." The writings of the eminent scholars who have led or championed that skeptical crusade will be searched in vain for proof of acquaintance with the scheme of Divine prophecy, a scheme that can be traced, like a silver thread, through all the Scriptures. And still more remarkable is their neglect of the typology of scripture. which is so closely allied with prophecy. Indeed, their "learned" writings are notable examples of exegesis on the text-card system. These Critics are like men who empty the works of a watch into a bowl, and then, after examining them in detail, arrive at the sapient conclusion that they present no proof of unity or design! The aphorism that "truth is one" applies unreservedly to Holy Writ. But if we read it on the text-card system we lose all sense of its "hidden harmony."

We cannot intelligently apprehend what God has revealed about the future if we are ignorant or unmindful of His revelation respecting the past and the present. We need, for example, to recognize the dual character of this "Christian Age." For, as already noticed, the root error of the Apostasy of Christendom is the failure to distinguish between the Professing Church, the administration of which is committed to man, and the true Church which Christ is building. The Professing Church is for earth and time, whereas the spiritual Church stands related to eternity and heaven. The truth respecting it is a "mystery" of the Christian revelation. And its temporary connection with earth will cease at that Coming of the Lord, which is another of the "mystery" truths revealed in the Epistles of the N.T.

In this, its higher aspect, the present dispensation is not within the purview of the earlier Scriptures.

And, viewed in relation to earth and time, it is an interlude in the great drama of prophecy as unfolded in those Scriptures. To rule out in this way some two thousand years of human history will seem neither startling nor strange, if we remember that, with God, a thousand years are "as yesterday when it is past, or as a watch in the night." And as regards the past we must keep in view the Divine plan of the ages. The Adamic dispensation was brought to an end by the judgment of the Flood; and the Noachic was marked by the Babylonian apostasy, in which the primeval revelation was utterly corrupted. An apostasy so subtly adapted to our fallen nature that even Evangelical Christianity is leavened by it. God thereupon took up Abraham and his race to be His agents and witnesses upon earth, and "unto them were committed the oracles of God." But the nation of Israel proved false to that trust; and instead of being light-bearers to the world, they proudly claimed a monopoly of Divine favor.

The Holy Temple, designed to be "a house of prayer for all nations," they regarded as their own house, and ended by making it "a den of thieves." Here, then, we have the clue to a right reading of the 11th chapter of Romans. It is a chapter of cardinal importance to the student of prophecy, but it is much neglected. And the Apostle's warning to us Gentiles not to be "wise in our own conceits" is practically ignored, as witness the figment that "the Christian Church" has ousted Israel from the olive tree position. The teaching of the chapter is explicit, that Gentiles are wild olive branches, "grafted, contrary to nature, into a good olive tree," the natural branches being Israelite. But they are only branches. For the allegory of the olive tree points back to the Abrahamic covenant and promise. And it is not as "members of the Church" that we are grafted into it, but as Gentiles, who, in virtue of faith, are become "children of Abraham." In the true Church there is neither Jew nor Gentile. Neither is there in the Vine, which represents a vital relationship with Christ, to be manifested by fruit-bearing.

And this chapter teaches emphatically that the present age is not only parenthetical but, in its earthly aspect, abnormal. And further, that as Israel was cut off because of unbelief, so the Professing Church of this age will be cut off. And then "There shall come out of Zion the Deliverer, and He shall turn away ungodliness from Jacob. And so all Israel shall be saved" (v. 26). Not "every Israelite," but Israel as a nation. For this chapter does not deal with the position and destiny of individuals, but with national and dispensational distinctions and changes.

Neither does it deal with Churches in the sense of our English word "denominations," but with the Professing Church on earth as a whole. For Scripture recognizes only two Churches, namely, the Church the Body of Christ, which, when complete, will be manifested in heavenly glory; and the Professing Church, "the outward frame of so-called Christendom," now drifting to its "fearful end." Even with knowledge of its evil history and present condition, we can form no adequate conception of what it will become when all true Christians are called away to heaven, and the influence of the Holy Spirit is no longer felt. But with awe we ponder the words of the Apocalyptic vision, that when the day of its judgment comes all heaven will ring with Hallelujahs, and the wonderful Beings who sit around the throne will fall upon their faces in adoring worship as they join in the refrain, "Hallelujah, Amen" "All Israel shall be saved." "And if the casting away of them was the reconciling of the world, what shall the receiving of them be but life from the dead!"

The cemetery condition in which Christendom will leave the world shall give place to the life and gladness of a summer garden! For when the People of the Covenant have been regenerated in the great revival foretold in prophecy, "the gospel of the Kingdom will be preached in all the world." And the result of their testimony will be the in-numerable multitude of earth's great Feast of Ingathering "out of all nations and kindreds and peoples and tongues." Let us then shake free not only from the errors, but from the mean pettiness of Latin theology on this great subject. One of the most popular of its accredited exponents in our own day describes the present age as "the last great eon of God's dealings with mankind," Could we but realize aright the significance of the Ministry and Death of Christ in God's purposes for earth, we might be tempted to declare that this age of ours is the first great eon of the unfolding of those purposes. And the statement, though unwarranted, would not be so flagrantly false as is the "pandemonium and conflagration" theory of this theology.

If only we knew more of God, and if we realized that earth's history runs its course in open view of all the great intelligences of heaven, the mysteries of both the past and the present might perchance seem less perplexing. And we should be led with eagerness to scan the prophecies still unfulfilled, to find there that this sin-cursed earth is yet to be a scene of blessedness and peace -- all that we should expect a God of infinite goodness and power to make it:

> "When a King, in kingly glory, Such as Earth has never known, Shall assume the righteous scepter, Claim and wear the holy crown."

Let us then, with the intelligent enthusiasm of faith, take our stand by the side of the inspired Apostle as, surveying this glorious vista of the Divine "plan of the ages," be exclaims, "0 the depth of the riches both of the wisdom and knowledge of God! How unsearchable are His judgments, and His ways past finding out!" But no intelligent student of these prophecies, and very specially of this eleventh chapter of Romans, can fail to recognize that before they can be realized there must be "a change of dispensation" as definite and drastic as that which was signalized by the call of Abraham, and again by the "casting away" of Israel, and the welcoming of Gentile slum-dwellers, and tramps of the highways, to partake of God's great supper of salvation. The reader of these pages, therefore, will appreciate their second title, and the prominence here given to the Coming of the Lord. It is not intended to suggest that "the hope of the Church" is within the scope of the Hebrew Scriptures. But the realization of that hope will usher in the age to which the great field of unfulfilled prophecy pertains. And therefore it provides the only standpoint from which that field can be surveyed in a true perspective.

CHAPTER 10

Three Future Comings of Christ

As noticed in preceding pages, there will be not less than three future Comings of Christ.

(1) That Coming by which this Christian dispensation of the reign of grace and the heavenly Church will be brought to an end;

(2) "the Coming of the Son of Man," in fulfillment of Messianic prophecy, to bring deliverance and blessing to His earthly people; and

(3) His Coming to judgment in a far distant future, at the close of the kingdom dispensation. But though the Coming of Christ is the hope of His people in every age, Theology gives us nothing but the "Second Advent" of His coming to judgment; and thus disposes, not only of the Christian's hope in the present dispensation, but of Israel's hope in the dispensation which is to follow it.

For while Christianity is based upon the teaching of Holy Scripture, "the Christian religion" depends largely upon the teaching of the Latin Fathers. And before the era of the great Patristic theologians "the hope of the Church" had already been forgotten; and Messianic prophecy had been so perverted or "spiritualized" as to shut out Israel's hope altogether.

But here a question of extreme importance claims attention. The saints of the Apostolic age were taught to live "in constant expectation of the Lord's return." How then is the delay of nineteen centuries to be accounted for? The Infidel's answer is that the Apostolic teaching was false. And some Christians would have us believe that, although the saints were divinely taught "to live looking for that blessed hope," it was settled by a Divine decree that the Lord would not come until long centuries had run their course. If these be the alternative solutions of the problem, most of us will take sides with the Infidel.

For though the loss of the Epistles would be a disaster, it would be infinitely worse to charge the God of truth with flagrant untruthfulness of a kind that would not be tolerated in our fellow-men. But we reject both alternatives with scorn. Some, again, would tell us that owing to the evil history of the Church on earth, even from the earliest times, the promise is cancelled, and the hope it engendered is lost. But though God is often said to have "repented" in regard to threatened judgments, Scripture records no instance of His failing to fulfill a promise of blessing.

Many a case, however, can be cited where the fulfillment was delayed because of unfaithfulness or sin on the part of His people. And does not this suggest the right solution of our difficulty? But if the Lord delays His Coming until "the Church" is what it ought to be, is not the promise practically cancelled? Yes; but it was not to the Church that He gave the promise, but to His elect people scattered throughout the Church. And nowhere is it given more explicitly than in the very Scriptures which foretell the Church's apostasy and doom. Plain words are needed here.

For in these days, when the Protestant spirit is waning in our land, there is no influence, perhaps, more harmful to Christian life than the prevalent superstitious and errors respecting "the outward frame of Christendom," "the Christian Church," as it is called. Our position in it and our attitude toward it ought to be akin to that which the Lord taught His disciples to maintain toward "the Jewish Church." They were in it, and yet, in a real sense, not of it. For though Divine in its origin and as to its responsibilities, it had apostatized. It was, in fact, "the world" of His prayer on their behalf (John xvii. 16). And as Bishop Westcott wrote of "the Christian Church," the world got into it in the fourth century, and has never since been got out of it. The crisis to which he referred was, presumably, the Conversion of Constantine. When wolves are about, the sheep keep near to the shepherd. And so, till then, the danger of persecution kept the Christians near to the Lord. But the century which followed was marked by such apostasy that, even in the sphere of morals, "the Christian Church" sank to the level of the heathen world.

The account given of it in Salvian's celebrated treatise on "Providence," written in the middle of the fifth century, is appalling. Here are two typical sentences from it:- "A very few excepted who flee from evil, what else is almost every assembly of Christians but a sink of vices. . . . I put it now to the conscience of all Christians whether it be not so, that you will hardly find one who is not addicted to some of the vices and crimes which I have mentioned; or rather, who is it that is not guilty of all? (Footnote: *full extracts in "The Bible or the Church"*)

The first Divine warning which Scripture gives of the apostasy of the Church is the Apostle's Paul's address to the Elders of Ephesus (Acts 20:29, 30). And it is an extremely significant fact that while his Epistles written prior to that epoch were addressed to Churches, his "Captivity" Epistles were addressed to "the Saints at Ephesus"; "the Saints at Phiippi;" "the Saints at Colosse." In these evil days we need to hold fast the great truth which Bishop John Ryle, of Liverpool, championed so fearlessly, that "there is only one true Church," the spiritual fold which includes only those who are Christians in the deeper sense. His Christian Leaders of the Last Century is, incidentally, a grave indictment of "the Christian Churches" in our land. He shows, indeed, that at that epoch they were the enemies of Christ and of His people.

When toward the end of the eighteenth century William Carey sought to excite interest in missions to the heathen, among his brethren in the Baptist Ministry, he was put down as a troublesome faddist. For "if the heathen were elect, they would be saved without their help; and if God wished them to send out missionaries He would renew the gift of tongues." And when Carey and Thomas sailed for India in June, 1793, they went out as emissaries, not of "the Christian Church," but of a dozen Baptist Ministers-

"troublesome faddists "-assembled in the low roofed back parlour of Widow Wallis, at Kettering, in October, 1792. Thus was launched, to quote Sydney Smith's sneer, by a few 'consecrated cobblers,' the first English mission to the heathen in India.' If the men who took the initiative in work of this kind had waited for "the Christian Church "to promote missions to the heathen, the heathen would possibly be still unevangelized. For even the Church Missionary Society was the offspring of the despised "Clapham Sect." The meeting at which it was founded was held in neither Westminster Abbey nor St. Paul's, but in a hired room in a poor sort of city inn. And it was not till forty years afterwards that Ecclesiastical dignitaries accorded it their patronage. For by that time all the Churches had begun to feel the influence of the Evangelical revival of the early decades of last century.

Still deeper and far more widespread was the influence of the revival which marked the middle of the century. But no sooner did the spiritual power of that revival begin to wane than a new apostasy set in.

And as the result our National Church has been so thoroughly corrupted by Romanizing influences that it is no longer Protestant, and the great Evangelical Party is but a memory of the past. And all our British Churches have been leavened with the Kultur of that German infidelity which has reduced that nation morally to the level of savages.

But what bearing has all this upon the truth of the Lord's Coming? It is owing to a false estimate of "the Church" that so many devout Christians neglect that truth, seeing that it is ignored in all our doctrinal standards. It will be said, perhaps, that it has no place in the "dogmatic theology" of the Epistles. True, for it is a fact of great significance that the Coming of the Lord is never mentioned as a doctrine that needed to be expounded, but only as a truth with which every Christian was supposed to be familiar.

And the reason of this is clear. For the very first day on which a convert was privileged to enter a Christian assembly he heard the words, "As often as ye eat this bread, and drink the cup, ye proclaim the Lord's death till He come." And if "unlearned in doctrine," he might well ask, "But has He not come?" and then all would be explained to him; and ever afterwards, as week by week he heard those charter words, the hope of the Coming would be inseparably linked with the atoning death of Christ.

But with Christians generally all this is now forgotten, and the Lord's Supper points only back to Calvary. And it is too commonly associated with "the cult of the Crucifix," which reaches the Pagan level in "the reservation of the Sacrament" and "the Mass." Indeed, there are many, even among spiritual Christians, who habitually speak of the Supper as "remembering the Lord's death." We do thus "proclaim the Lord's death"; but the vital and essential element in the sacred rite is that to which the Lord's own words give emphasis: "This do in remembrance of ME" --not a dead Christ, but an absent Savior and Lord.

If then, shaking free from every false or superstitious estimate of "the Church" and its theology, the Lord's Supper regained its right place in Christian thought and Christian experience, the truth of the Coming would be restored to the place it held in Apostolic days; and a vague sort of intellectual faith in a "Second Advent" in a vastly distant future, would give place to a real heart-belief in the Lord's return, as a present hope, to cheer and comfort us in sorrow, and to influence character and conduct in our daily life.

Of days in Israel when their religious leaders failed them it was written, "Then they that feared the Lord spake often one to another; and the Lord listened, and He heard it; and a book of remembrance was written before Him." And in these days of ours let us remember that it was not "the Church" or its leaders that promoted missions to the heathen, but a few lightly-esteemed Christians who were fired with the enthusiasm of faith in God. And if even a very few spiritual Christians in every place would begin to "speak often one to another" about the Coming of the Lord they would soon come together to pray for His return. And from such small beginnings, it may be that, for the first time in the history of Christendom, companies of His people shall be found meeting together to claim 'the fulfillment of His promise, "Surely I am coming quickly," and to pray the prayer which He Himself has given us, "Even so, come Lord Jesus." THE END

FORGOTTEN TRUTHS

Sir Robert Anderson

Second Edition

First Edition originally published January 1, 1914

Note from the publisher

This book was originally published in 1914, but its information is still very useful to help the Bible student understand difficult passages.

The footnotes have been moved to the end of each paragraph.

PREFACE
TO THE SECOND EDITION

THE early demand for a new edition of "Forgotten Truths" gives proof that truths which have been let slip by so many are still cherished by not a few. The only adverse criticism the book has evoked is that which was anticipated in the closing pages of Chap. 12.

In the early years of my Christian life I was greatly perplexed and distressed by the supposed position that the plain and simple words of such Scriptures as John 3:16, 1 John 2:2, 1 Timothy 2:6 were not true, save in a cryptic sense understood only by the initiated. For, I was told, the overshadowing truth of Divine sovereignty in election barred our taking them literally. But half a century ago a friend of those days - the late Dr. Horatius Bonar - delivered me from this strangely prevalent error. He taught me that truths may seem to us irreconcilable only because our finite minds cannot understand the Infinite; and we must never allow our faulty apprehension of the eternal counsels of God to hinder unquestioning faith in the words of Holy Scripture.

Nor was this a plausible effort to evade the special difficulty raised by a misuse of the great truth of election; for a kindred mystery permeates our whole existence. We are conscious of possessing a free and independent will which enables us to turn hither and thither as we please, and to do good or evil. Were it otherwise, indeed, the Divine judgment of the sinner would be unjust. And yet, when we review the consequences of our conduct, we recognize the hand of God. True it is that we think of Him only when the consequences are serious; but, as the Lord explicitly taught, His sovereignty declares itself even in the fall of a sparrow.

All this has its counterpart in relation to the promise of the Coming. The believer and the infidel are agreed that in Apostolic times the saints were taught to regard the Lord's return as a hope that might be realized during their lifetime. But now we are asked to acknowledge that the infidel is right in maintaining that this was entirely a mistake! For, it is argued, the Lord cannot come till "the number of His elect" is complete. And Ephesians 1:4 is construed to mean that at some epoch in time, prior to 4004 B.C. (or whatever date be fixed for "the foundation of the world"), people now living were made beneficiaries of God's favor. It follows, therefore, that, as "the number of the elect" was not complete prior to this twentieth century of our era, the Advent could not have taken place at any period in the past; and possibly the thirtieth century may dawn before the promise is fulfilled! And when in amazement we seek for some explanation of the words, "Surely I am coming quickly," we are told that "with the Lord a thousand years are as one day" (2 Peter 3:8.). But does any one really imagine that there is a celestial timepiece with a thousand-year dial! Is it not clear as light from the language of these and kindred Scriptures, such as Psalm 90:4, that eternity is God's domain? Therefore is it that His judgments are unsearchable and His ways past finding out. For eternity is not unlimited time, but the antithesis of time; whereas time is the law of our being, "the condition under which all created things exist" (Trench, Synonyms).

Those who put a special meaning on certain words in Gospel texts can plead with truth that these words are sometimes used in a restricted sense. But no plea of the kind is tenable here. "I am surely coming quickly":" Yet a very little while and the Coming One will come, and will not delay." These words are too definite to admit of any second meaning; and to refuse to take them literally is equivalent to challenging their truth. But how then can we explain the fact that they are still unfulfilled? A solution of that most perplexing difficulty is supplied by the following pages.

    Robert Anderson

CHAPTER 1

SOME QUESTIONS RAISED

THE lapse of time has not effaced from my memory the details of a conversation of many years ago with a liberal-minded and cultured Jewish Rabbi. He introduced himself by telling me that he was a student of the New Testament, and that my friend, the then Chief Rabbi, had recommended one of my expository books to his attention. "We regard Jesus as one of the greatest of our Rabbis," was one of his opening remarks. And he added, "It was not he that founded Christianity, but your Paul." I astonished him by replying that beneath his assertion there lay a truth which the theology of Christendom had let slip. For the words of the Lord Jesus (1) were explicit: "I am not sent but to the lost sheep of the House of Israel"; "Salvation is of the Jews." In this connection I cited also the Apostle's words, that "Christ was a minister of the circumcision for the truth of God, to confirm the promises made unto the Fathers, and that the Gentiles might glorify God for His mercy." (Romans 15:8) And this I explained by reference to the Lord's parable of the great supper. "You were the invited guests," I said, "for to you pertained the Fathers and the promises, whereas the Gentiles are beholden to uncovenanted mercy. But though by nature the waifs and strays of the highways and the streets, grace has given us a place of special favor and nearness to God."

> 1] Throughout our conversation he always spoke of Him as Jesus; and I as the Lord Jesus.

The pleasant tenor of a prolonged conversation was interrupted at one point by an outburst about "the persecutions and cruelties his nation had suffered from the Christian religion." This evoked a no less indignant outburst on my part at his confounding the religion of Christendom with the Christianity of the New Testament. I assured him that the best Christian theologians of our own time were free from the ignorance which in other days claimed for "the Christian Church" (2) all the promises of the Hebrew Scriptures, leaving nothing for Israel but the threatened judgments. And I exemplified my statement by quoting Dean Alford's scathing words about the evil history and predicted doom of "the Christian Church.": I said that while in the past the Christians seem to have skipped the 11th chapter of Romans, nowadays we studied it. We recognized, therefore, that the people of the Abrahamic Covenant were "the natural branches" of the olive tree which symbolizes the position of testimony and blessing upon earth, and that they would yet be restored to the place they had lost by unbelief; "for the gifts and calling of God are without repentance." (Romans 11:13-29)

2] New Testament Commentary, Matthew 12:43-45.

]This is but an outline of a discussion which ended, as it had begun, in a most amicable tone and spirit, my companion repeatedly assuring me of the interest and surprise my words excited in his mind. But the questions raised and the truths involved are far too large and too important for treatment here in this incidental fashion; and I proceed to offer a more definite and systematic statement of them.

CHAPTER 2

ETERNAL WORD OF GOD

"O THE depth of the riches both of the wisdom and knowledge of God! how unsearchable are His judgments, and His ways past finding out!" (Romans 11:33)

Such was the burst of praise that rose from the heart of the inspired Apostle as he realized that the seeming failure of all that Hebrew prophets had foretold of blessing upon earth at the coming of Messiah had been made the occasion of a new revelation, which should lead up to the fulfillment of all their God-breathed words.

"The seeming failure," I say advisedly. For though theologians have written "The enlargement of the Church" over such Scriptures as Isaiah 54, 60, 66, no sane and sensible person will pretend that there exists today, or has ever existed in the past, a condition of things on earth that could be accepted as the fulfillment of these prophecies. And to suppose that such a condition of things will result from the influences at work in the present economy betokens sheer blindness and folly. The time has come for plain speaking on this subject. "Clear the decks," is the first order given when a warship prepares for action. And the vagaries of old-fashioned "orthodox" exegesis are top-hamper that grievously embarrasses the defense of Holy Scripture in these days when its Divine authority is so virulently attacked. As the inspired Apostle declared at Pentecost, "the times of the restitution of all things" — or, in other words, the times when all things will be put right — are the burden of Hebrew prophecy from Moses to Malachi, (Acts 3:19) and the fulfillment of these prophecies awaits the return of Christ.

The fact is plain to all who will use their brains that the condition of Christendom, and of the world at large, differs essentially from what is portrayed and promised in the visions of the Hebrew Seers. But these "holy men of God spake as they were moved by the Holy Ghost," (2 Peter 1:21) and no word of God can fail. No lapse of time affects it; for in His sight a thousand years are as a forgotten yesterday, or as a watch in the night. (Psalm 90:4) Thus it is that He would teach us that time is but a law of human thought, and that eternity is His domain.

Therefore, while unbelief dismisses these prophecies as old-world classics, the Christian accepts them as divine - the Word of God, "which liveth and abideth for ever." And this being so, chronology has no bearing on the vital question here at issue. For we are "not ignorant of this one thing, that one day is with the Lord as a thousand years, and a thousand years as one day." (2 Peter 3:8) "Today is the third day since these things were done," was the despairing lament of the disciples on the road to Emmaus; but their unbelief brought upon them the Lord's rebuke, "O fools, and slow of heart to believe all that the prophets have spoken." And when the skeptical pundits would shake our faith by reminding us that the prophets' words are still unfulfilled after the lapse of well-nigh three thousand years, we exclaim, "Three thousand years! Then today is the third day since these things were spoken!"

Spiritual discernment and ordinary intelligence are needed in the study of Holy Scripture. Spirituality is the prime essential, for spiritual truths are spiritually discerned; but common sense, to use the popular phrase, will generally save us from the follies of false exegesis. And false exegesis, I repeat, affords a vantage-ground for skeptical attacks on Scripture. To give an illustration of this, extremely apt in the circumstances of the day, I will quote a passage from Professor Tyndall's famous address on "Science and Man." Referring to the "Angels' Song," he exclaimed, "Look to the East at the present moment, as a comment on the promise of peace on earth and good will toward men. The promise is a dream ruined by the experience of eighteen centuries." The answer to this taunt is full and clear. The great birth in Bethlehem heralded the fulfillment of all that God had promised of blessing to the world. "The times of the restitution of all things," to quote the Apostle Peter's words again, were to come with the advent of Christ. And now "the Coming One" had come. Why then were not the promised blessings realized? Why, but because of His rejection. "His own received Him not," and "the world knew Him not." The Christ was crucified on Calvary. And when the Apostles were divinely commissioned to proclaim to His murderers that a national repentance would bring Him back to earth, with the fulfillment of every blessing of which their prophets spoke, the response made by that guilty people was to persecute the ministers of this great reconciliation and hound them to death. But it may be asked, Has the sin of man changed the purposes of God? Most assuredly not. But, on account of that sin, the fulfillment of the Divine purposes his been postponed.

This then is the answer which Scripture gives to the skeptic's taunt. But very different are the conflicting answers which "old-fashioned orthodoxy" offers. For some would have us believe that "the millennium" will result from the preaching of the Gospel in the present dispensation. And by others we are told that all we have to look for is "the end of the world," when the Lord will come to take His people to Himself, and judgment fire will engulf this sin cursed earth. The former view was popular in the early days of the nineteenth-century revival; but in the present state of Christendom in general, and of the Churches of the Reformation in particular, anyone who clings to it today must be either a mystic or a fossil And if the other view be accepted, the closing words of the 11th of Romans must be dismissed as the wildest rhapsody; for the unsearchable judgments of Divine wisdom and knowledge are thus made to find their realization in a pandemonium to be followed by a bonfire.

This "spiritualizing," as it is called, of the Hebrew Scriptures has given the Jew a fair ground for rejecting the Christian's appeal to the Messianic prophecies. And thus, as Adolf Saphir says with sorrow, "It is out of the arsenal of the orthodox that the weapons have been taken with which the very fundamental truths of the Gospel have been assailed." And he goes on to show how "this spiritualistic interpretation paved the way for Rationalism and Neology."

Let us then be done with it once for all; and rejecting absolutely the popular canon of exegesis, that Holy Scripture never says what it means, and never means what it says, let us learn with humility and reverence to accept all the Divine words at their face value. When the Lord declared that not a jot or tittle of the law shall fail of its fulfillment, He was speaking, not of the decalogue, but, as the context indicates, of the Hebrew Scriptures as a whole. Remembering, then, that these Scriptures are the Word of Him with whom both the past and the future are a living present, let us read them with the settled conviction that every promise, and every prophecy, relating to earth and the earthly people must be fulfilled as definitely as were the seemingly unbelievable prophecies and promises about the birth and death of Christ.

But on this subject our theology, so far from reflecting "the wisdom and knowledge of God," partakes of the ignorance and the errors of the Patristic theologians. Plain words, I repeat, are needed here. For the writings of the Latin Fathers afford a vantage-ground both for Romish attacks upon the citadel of Divine truth, and for the insidious efforts of German skepticism to undermine its very foundations. It is noteworthy that though the writers of the New Testament, one and all, were men who, like Timothy, had known the Hebrew Scriptures from infancy, (1) the Patristic theologians were converts from Paganism. And having regard to their comparative want of acquaintance with the Old Testament, it is not strange, perhaps, that in the then condition of the Jewish people, crushed apparently beyond hope of recovery by the judgments that had overwhelmed them, the belief prevailed that God had "cast away His people whom He foreknew." But it is both strange and sad that such a belief should still survive in these enlightened days of ours. In proof that it does survive, appeal might be made to many a standard work; but for my present purpose it will suffice to quote the following sentence from the prolific pen of a writer of the highest repute as a popular theologian: "The divine and steady light of history first made clear to the Church that our Lord's prophetic warnings as to

His return applied primarily to the close of the Jewish dispensation, and the winding up of all the past, and the inauguration of the last great aeon of God's dealings with mankind." (2)

> 1] It is mere tradition that would exclude the Evangelist Luke from this category, and the facts outweigh the tradition.
>
> 2] Dean Farrar's Life and Work of St. Paul, vol. i. p. 598. The italics are mine. I shall have occasion to refer to this passage again with reference to the truth of the Coming.

If we are to recover truth which the Church, in its incipient apostasy, lost through following the human light of history, we must seek it by "the Divine and steady light" of Holy Writ. And that light will make clear to us that, like many another Scripture, the promise to Abraham has a twofold aspect. It pointed to Christ and the redemption of Calvary; but it still awaits its secondary fulfillment through the agency of the covenant people. "In thy seed shall all the nations of the earth be blessed." (Genesis 22:18.) (3) The spiritually intelligent Bible student accepts that promise as the Word of the Lord, that endureth for ever, and he knows that it will be literally fulfilled. And he knows also, that this Christian dispensation is not "the last great aeon of God's dealings with mankind," but rather a beginning of what, in His unsearchable counsels, He has in store for the blessing of this sin-blighted world.

> 3] That it has a secondary meaning is clearly indicated by the 17th verse.

That glorious vista of future blessing, which filled so large a place in the visions of the Hebrew Seers, was but the unfolding of the prophecy of the sacred calendar. For the Passover is only the first of the great Festivals which typify the harvest of redemption. This present dispensation with its sheaf of the first-fruits, (4) the true, the heavenly Church, is to be followed by the Feast of Pentecost, when Israel reunited - the two wave loaves of the typical ritual - will be restored to Divine favor. And beyond these spring-time festivals there comes the harvest-home of redemption upon earth, in the fulfillment of the great Feast of Tabernacles, when unnumbered multitudes of the saved shall know and serve the Lord. This is no "cunningly devised fable," no mere dream of a visionary; it is a summary of what Scripture plainly teaches. And, rejecting the unworthy figment that earth is merely a recruiting-ground for heaven, to be given up to fire when the Church has been safely garnered, faith looks out with joy upon this glorious vista of the future, when the Abrahamic promise shall receive complete fulfillment, and Christ "shall see of the travail of His soul, and shall be satisfied."

> 4] In its highest fulfillment the sheaf of the first-fruits is Christ personally; but dispensationally it typifies the redeemed of this Christian age, "a kind of first-fruits of His creatures" (James 1:18).

It is in this spirit and on these principles that the present inquiry shall proceed. And the nature and scope of the inquiry may be stated thus - "What light does Scripture throw upon the abnormal condition of things on earth during this age, when "the people of the covenant" are in rejection?" And what are the distinctive truths of Christianity, or, in other words, the special "mystery" truths of the New Testament revelation? As this word "mystery" will occur again and again in the following pages, it may be well to explain that it is here employed in its Scriptural acceptation, as signifying "not a thing unintelligible, but what lies hidden and secret till made known by the revelation of God." (5) Or as Dr. Sanday gives it, "something which up to the time of the Apostles had remained secret, but had then been made known by Divine intervention."

> 5] These words are quoted from Dr. Bloomfield's Greek Testament. "Mysteries of the faith" he again defines as "certain verities hitherto quite unknown, and which could be derived from no other source but a Divine revelation."

CHAPTER 3

BLESSING FOR GENTILES

IN Lord Beaconsfield's Life of Lord George Bentinck there is a pathetically interesting chapter about the treatment meted out to the Jews by Christendom. He attributes their persistent rejection of Christianity to the fact that it was by a campaign of persecution and outrage that "the Christian religion" sought to force itself upon their acceptance. His own Jewish ancestors, as we know, were driven out of Spain by the Inquisition. "Is it wonderful, therefore," he might well ask, "that a great portion of the Jewish race should not believe in the most important portion of the Jewish religion?" For thus he correctly describes the atonement of Calvary. The "orthodox" figment that Christ came to found a new religion was in effect the gravamen of the charge on which the Apostle Paul was arraigned by his Jewish persecutors. For preaching a new religion was an offence against Roman law. And the Apostle's defence was an emphatic repudiation of that charge. In his ministry among them, he declared, he taught "nothing but what the prophets and Moses did say should come." (Acts 26:22, 23) Blessing for Gentiles is not a New Testament truth. It was assured by the promise to Abraham, and explicitly foretold in Hebrew prophecy. But that "the people of the covenant" should lose nationally the privileged position of earthly testimony is a New Testament "mystery," (Romans 11:25) albeit Christians in general regard it as a matter of course. The 11th chapter of Romans teaches explicitly that the present economy is abnormal and temporary. For the olive tree is not the symbolism of a heavenly calling, but of the place of earthly testimony. And the "natural branches" of the olive tree are the covenant people.

But were not the natural branches broken off? Such is the false belief of Christendom religion. The teaching of Scripture is that "some of the branches" were broken off, and that, "contrary to nature," wild olive branches (i.e. Gentiles) have been "grafted in among them." But the root of the olive remains, and the root is the people of the Abrahamic covenant. (Romans 11:17-24) For "to them pertaineth the covenants." (Romans 9:4) This cannot be evaded by the plea that, when the Epistle to the Romans was written, the "Pentecostal Dispensation" was still current, and therefore a place of repentance was still open to the Jews. For the very same principle obtains with reference to the heavenly Church, the full revelation of which is found in "the Captivity Epistles." Gentile Christians seem to regard the Church, the Body of Christ, as theirs in a peculiar sense, whereas in Ephesians 3:6 the Apostle represents it as a signal proof of Divine grace "that the Gentiles are fellow-heirs (with Israelites) and fellow-members of the body."

Appealing to the Savior's intercessory prayer upon the Cross as securing Divine forgiveness for Israel for crucifying the Messiah, Lord Beaconsfield rightly challenges the received belief that the destruction of Jerusalem was a judgment for that greatest of all human sins. And yet that it was a Divine judgment is unquestionable. And if not for the crucifixion, how can it be accounted for. Here Lord Beaconsfield entirely misses the significance of the facts, and the nature of the question to which the facts give rise. It is a question, moreover, of exceptional interest, and of great importance in relation to the present inquiry. And a clew to the solution of it will be found in the events of the Babylonian era.

Because of national apostasy, the Divine judgment of the Servitude to Babylon fell upon Judah in the third year of the reign of King Jehoiakim. But owing to their continued impenitence, the severer judgment of the "Captivity" followed, nine years after the "Servitude" began. Even this, however, failed to move them; and in the seventeenth year of the "Servitude," their persistent obduracy brought on them the third, and far more terrible, judgment of the seventy years' "Desolations." That era began on the day when, for the third time, the Babylonian army invested Jerusalem; and the capture and burning of the city followed. (See Appendix 1.)

A national repentance after the "Servitude" began would not have canceled that judgment. Nor would a repentance after the people were carried into captivity have brought them back to their land. But all further chastisement would have been averted; and when the seventy years of the Servitude ended, and the decree of Cyrus permitted their return, they would have found their city intact and the holy temple still standing. Now mark the parallel between all this and the events of the Apostolic age. The proto-martyr Stephen was the messenger sent after the banished king to say, "We will not have this man to reign over us." His murder was the nation's response to the Pentecostal promise that a national repentance would bring Christ back to them. But repentance even after that murder, though it would not have restored them to the privileged position which they had forfeited, would have saved them from further punishment. And the parallel may be carried further still. For forty years before the city was captured and burned by Nebuchadnezzar, the prophet's warning voice was never silent in their midst [1] So for forty years before Jerusalem was taken and destroyed by Titus, the gospel was preached unceasingly in every place where Hebrews congregated.

> 1] Jeremiah prophesied from the thirteenth year of Josiah (627 B.C.) until the fall of Jerusalem in the eleventh year of Zedekiah (587 B.C.). See Jeremiah 1:2, 3.

During all the forty years of Jeremiah's ministry, as the chronicler records, God in mercy waited, "because He had compassion on His people and on His dwelling place. But they mocked the messengers of God and despised His words, and misused His prophets, until the wrath of the Lord arose against His people, till there was no remedy." (2 Chronicles 36:15, 16) These words might have been repeated without the slightest variation with reference to the forty years that elapsed between the ministry of Christ and the time of that awful judgment, when Jerusalem was sacked and burned by the Roman army.

"They misused His prophets." The murder of Stephen was due to no sudden burst of passion; and their Roman governors had no share in it. It was the execution of a judicial sentence passed by the great Council of the nation. Not even the Crucifixion itself was more unequivocally the act of "the Commonwealth of Israel"; and the inspired narrative which records it marks its deep significance by recording as its sequel the call of the Apostle of the Gentiles.

But God is "abundant in mercy," and though Israel thus forfeited the national blessing which a national repentance would have brought them, the Apostle of the Gentiles was charged with a special mission to the Jews of the dispersion; [2] and in every place his first appeal was to the synagogue. And can we doubt that if his testimony had been accepted, God, who would have spared Sodom for the sake of even ten righteous, would have certainly spared Jerusalem? But in all the wide circuit of the Apostle's ministry, there was not a single provincial Sanhedrin or local synagogue that accepted the proffered mercy. Divine forbearance met with no response. "There was no remedy." So at last the judgment fell. Amid circumstances of unparalleled horror Jerusalem was destroyed, and the Jews were driven out as homeless wanderers from the land of their inheritance.

> 2] The Apostle Paul's commission to the Jews is generally overlooked: "the people and the Gentiles, unto whom I send thee" (Acts 26:17). "To both the people and the Gentiles; not the Gentiles only." Alford in loco.

Now but for that judgment the Jews would have remained in a position akin to that assigned to them in the Servitude to Babylon — a nation in vassalage to Gentile sovereignty, but with their own land and their own city. And it is a fact of extreme importance that this was their actual condition when the Epistle to the Romans was written. But ignoring all this, the 11th chapter of that Epistle, which ought to be read in the clear light of Holy Scripture, came to be misread in the dim and discoloured light of human inferences from human history. The destruction of Jerusalem was supposed to be the end of Jewish hopes and Jewish story. And as Romans was written prior to the time of that disaster, the 11th chapter of the Epistle was taken as cancelled; and Old Testament prophecy relating to the future glory of Israel was "spiritualized" to mean the present glory of "the Church."

And this explains a fact which Protestantism struggles to evade, namely, that the writings of the Fathers laid the foundations on which the fabric of the apostasy of Christendom was reared. For the figment that "God has cast away His people whom He foreknew," [3] and therefore that the present economy is the fulfillment of Hebrew prophecy and the realization of Divine purposes for earth, is in the warp and woof of the theology of Christendom. Hence the baneful superstitions about "the Christian Church" which are the secret of Rome's aggressive influence. There is never a Protestant drawn into that fold who is not the dupe of these superstitions. And even evangelical and spiritual Christians are corrupted by them; for they are so congenial to human nature that the exposure of them, not only by the Reformers, but by eminent divines of our own day, is generally ignored.

> 3] The A.V. makes the 15th verse of Romans 11 contradict verse 2, where a different, Greek word is used. And the R.V. is quite as unsatisfactory, for it uses a stronger phrase in ver. 15 than in ver. 2. (See The Oxford English Dictionary.) A garment befouled with filth is "thrown away," but a garment that impedes our movements is "thrown off" The word used in ver. 15 occurs in its verbal form in this very sense in Mark 10:50.

Blessing for Gentiles, I repeat, is not a New Testament revelation. Witness the words of the promise to Abraham and, as a Divine commentary upon that promise, the inspired prayer at the dedication of the Temple -"Moreover concerning the stranger, which is not of Thy people Israel, but is come from a far country for Thy great name's sake, and Thy mighty hand, and Thy stretched out arm; if they come and pray in this house; then hear Thou from the heavens, even from Thy dwelling place, and do according to all that the stranger calleth to Thee for; that all the people of the earth may know Thy name, and fear Thee." (2 Chronicles 6:32, Cf. 33; Isaiah 56:3-7)

But "the Jewish Church" was false to its trust, though not so grossly false as "the Christian Church" has proved. For while the Jew treated the Gentile as a pariah, Christendom has regarded Jews as enemies to be shunned, if not as vermin to be exterminated. Hence the fact that so few Gentiles came within the blessing during the old economy, and that, during the new, so few Jews have accepted Christ. "The name of God is blasphemed among the Gentiles through you" (Romans 2:24) was the scathing charge brought against "the Jewish Church" in its apostasy, and it is due to the deeper apostasy of "the Christian Church" that the name of Christ is blasphemed among the Jews.

But in modern times British Christianity has done not a little to clear itself from this reproach. And the question is germane to the present inquiry only in so far as it bears upon the character of the professing Church on earth. For Christian thought, even among Evangelicals, is leavened with the root error of the Roman Apostasy, namely, the confounding the true and heavenly Church, the Body of Christ, with "the Christian Church" on earth, or, to adopt Dean Alford's synonym for it, "the outward frame of so-called Christendom."

It is a sad proof that we have lapsed from the teaching of Scripture and the principles of the Reformation. With the Reformers "the Holy Catholic Church" was not an unholy alliance with all Christendom, but "the whole congregation of Christian people dispersed throughout the whole world." [4] Thus it was that they sought to break the entail of hideous guilt attaching to the historic Church. They had drunk deep of the spirit of the Apostle's words to the Ephesian elders in days of incipient apostasy "I commend you to God, and to the word of His grace, which is able to build you up, and to give you an inheritance among all them which are sanctified." (Acts 20:32.) [5] Let us then seek to follow their noble example; and clearing our minds of the prevalent superstitions about the Church on earth, let us take our stand with them upon Holy Scripture and the faithfulness of God. The next branch of our inquiry relates to other "mystery" truths of the New Testament revelation, which, no less than that of the present phase of the olive tree, are well-nigh forgotten. And the mystery of grace enthroned in heaven claims priority of notice.

> 4] 55th Canon of the Convention of 1603.
>
> 5] It is noteworthy that the Epistles to the Thessalonians, Corinthians, and Galatians are addressed to churches, whereas his Epistles after this date — Ephesians, Philippians, Colossians — are addressed to "the saints" in those places.

NOTE CHAPTER 3: THE ERAS OF SERVITUDE

THE Divine judgment of the 70 years' Servitude to Babylon fell in 606 B.C., which was the third year of King Jehoiakim, and the year before the accession of Nebuchadnezzar. The Jews refused to bow to the Divine judgment thus inflicted upon them, and in the ninth year of the Servitude they revolted (597 B.C.). This brought upon them the judgment of the Captivity. The Babylonian army again captured Jerusalem, and all "save the poorest sort of the people of the land" were deported to Chaldea. Jeremiah in Jerusalem, and Ezekiel among the captives, gave repeated warnings that continued impenitence would bring down a still fiercer judgment But, misled by promises of help from Egypt, the Jews again revolted in the tenth year of the Captivity; and, in fulfillment of prophetic warnings, their city was destroyed and their land laid desolate. "The Fast of Tebeth is still observed by the Jews of every land in commemoration of the day from which the era of the 70 years of "the Desolations" was reckoned, namely, the tenth day of the tenth month in the ninth year of King Zedekiah (589 B.C.). See Ezekiel 24:1, 2, and Kings 25:1.

Both the 70 years of the Servitude and the 62 years of the Captivity ended in 536 B.C., when the decree of Cyrus permitted the Jews to return to their own land. That decree expressly authorized the rebuilding of the Temple. But though the words of a Persian king were regarded as divine, that decree was thwarted by the local authorities in Judea until the reign of Darius Hystaspes. The explanation of this strange fact is that God would not permit the rebuilding of the Temple until the era of the Desolations ended.

The year in use both with the Jews and the Chaldeans was one of 860 days, the calendar being corrected by intercalation. And that this is the prophetic year is made plain both in Daniel and Revelation, 42 months being the equivalent of 1260 days. Now 70 years of 360 days contain 25,200 days; and the period between the 10th Tebeth 589 and the 24th Chisleu 520, when the foundation of the second Temple was laid (Haggai 2:18), was exactly 25,200 days.

It is very commonly assumed that Daniel's prayer of chapter 9 of his prophecy had reference to the 70 years of the Captivity, and that the 70 weeks were to end with the coming of Messiah. These blunders discredit many a learned writer. For there was no 70 years' captivity, and the period "unto Messiah the Prince" was not 70 weeks but 7 and 62 weeks. Daniel 9:2 states explicitly that it was the years of *the Desolations* that were the basis of the prayer and of the prophecy; and, as we have seen, these were prophetic years of 360 days. The era of the weeks was to date from the issue of a decree to rebuild Jerusalem. History records one such decree, and only one, viz. that of the month Nisan in the 20th year of Artaxerxes. And 69 sevens of prophetic years (173,800 days), measured from 1st Nisan, 445 B.C., end upon that fateful day in Passion week when, for the first and only time in His ministry, the Lord was publicly acclaimed as the Messiah the Prince. (Nehemiah 2; Luke 19:37 ff. Mark the words of verse 42: "If thou hadst known, even thou *in this day*, the things that belong to thy peace!")

But what then of the 70th week? Here it is that all this has an important bearing on the main subject of the preceding pages. As early as the days of Hippolytus, bishop and martyr, the belief prevailed that the fulfillment of Daniel's last week belongs to the future. And such was the view of Julius Africanus, "the father of Christian Chronologists." This, moreover, is entirely in keeping with the Lord's words in the synagogue of Nazareth; and it is definitely established by His words recorded in Matthew 24:15, with reference to Daniel 9:27. It is certain, moreover, that the 70th week has not been fulfilled in the past. For the 70th week begins with the covenant between the Jews and their last great patron, who becomes their last great persecutor. In the middle of the week he violates his treaty with them; and the latter half of the week (the 42 months, or 1260 days, of Daniel and Revelation) is the period of the Great Tribulation, which is to be followed immediately by the awful portents of the "Coming of the Son of Man," foretold in Isaiah 13:10 and Joel 2:31. (Matthew 24:29, and see verse 27.)

As already noticed, there will be a prolonged interval between those awful portents and the actual "Coming of the Son of Man." This is evident from the Lord's words in verses 36-44. And yet that Coming might have taken place within the lifetime of those to whom the words were addressed. But, as I have sought to show in preceding pages, all this has reference to Israel; and its fulfillment is in abeyance because of Israel's rejection during this Christian dispensation. The "Second Sermon on the Mount" will be fulfilled in every jot and tittle of it. But to throw it into hotch-potch with the distinctively Christian revelation entrusted to His Apostles after "the change of dispensation," modifying the language of both in the vain effort to make them harmonize — this displays neither spiritual intelligence nor reverence for Holy Scripture. [1]

> 1] The incidental questions involved in the chronology of the judgments of the exilic era, and of the seventy weeks, age too numerous and far too important to be treated in an Appendix note. But they are fully dealt with in *The Coming Prince; or, The Seventy Weeks of Daniel*, a book that has been before the public for thirty years, and is now in the ninth edition.

CHAPTER 4

GRACE ENTHRONED

IT is extraordinary that any student of Scripture can miss the clearly marked difference between the gospel of the opening clause of the Epistle to the Romans, and the gospel specified in the characteristically "Pauline" postscript at its close.

"Sojourners from Rome, both Jews and proselytes," were among the multitudes who heard the Divine amnesty proclaimed at Pentecost. And it was "to Jews only" that in those early days the word of that gospel was preached. (Acts 11:19) In Rome therefore, as elsewhere, Jews and proselytes constituted the nucleus and rallying centre of the Church. And we read the Epistle to the Romans amiss, if we fail to recognize what an important place its teaching accords to those Hebrew Christians. The word which had won them to Christ was that "gospel of God which He had promised afore by His prophets in the Holy Scriptures, concerning His Son who was born of the seed of David." Language could not more definitely indicate that it was the fulfillment of the hope of every true Israelite. Hence his words to the "Chief of the Jews" in Rome "For the hope of Israel I am bound with this chain." (Acts 28:20) And, as already noticed, his answer to the charge on which he was imprisoned was that his preaching to the Jews was based entirely on the Law and the Prophets. (Acts 26:22)

Such, then, was the burden of his ministry to his own people, a ministry he shared with all his brethren. But to Gentiles he preached a gospel which he had received by special revelation. And the specific purpose of his third visit to Jerusalem was to communicate that gospel to the other Apostles. (Galatians 2:2) In writing to Timothy he speaks of it as "the gospel of the glory of the blessed God, which was committed to my trust." It was the precious deposit which, on the eve of his martyrdom, he handed back, as it were, to the God who had entrusted it to him. (2 Timothy 1:12) And this is the "My gospel," of the postscript to his Epistle to the Romans. (Romans 16:25, 26) [1]

> 1] The same phrase, "My gospel," occurs also in ch. 2:16. How can anyone imagine that the Apostle would call the gospel his, save in the sense that it was the subject of a special revelation to himself!

Here are his words' "Now to Him that is able to stablish you according to my gospel, even the preaching of Jesus Christ according to a revelation of a mystery kept in silence through times eternal, but now manifested, and by prophetic writings according to the commandment of the Eternal God made known to all the nations unto obedience of faith" (or "obedience to the faith"). [2]

> 2] The first kai in this sentence is obviously epexegetic. If read otherwise, as in our English versions, the Apostle is made to distinguish between the gospel of Christ and a gospel of his own. And "the Scriptures of the Prophets" is a mistranslation that reduces the Apostle's words to an absurdity. For he is thus made to say that this "mystery" gospel was kept secret in all the past, and yet that it was plainly taught in the Old Testament Scriptures. The Greek is simple and clear. In ch. 1:2, the words are: "His prophets in holy writings" (i.e. the Old Testament Scriptures). In ch. 16:25, 26, the words are: "prophetic writings" (the inspired Scriptures of the New Testament). A prophet is "one who, moved by the Spirit of God, declares to men what he has received by inspiration" (Grimm's Lexicon). And therefore "prophetic" is equivalent to inspired; the element of foretelling the future is merely incidental.

It was in grace that God made promise to Abraham and granted him the covenant. But on the faithfulness of God it is that we rely to keep His promise and to fulfill His covenant. It is of his "kinsmen according to the flesh" that the Apostle speaks in the opening words of Romans 9. And of them, the Israelites, he says, "Whose is the adoption and the glory, and the covenants and the giving of the law, and the service of God and the promises; whose are the fathers, and of whom, as concerning the flesh, Christ came." And it was as "sons of the covenant" that the gospel was preached to them at Pentecost. (Acts 3:25) "The promise is to you and to your children," the Apostle testified; (Acts 2:39.) [3] for to them belonged the gospel of the covenant. But to the Gentiles, who were" strangers from the covenants of promise," (Ephesians 2:12) was preached the gospel of grace - the gospel of the "mystery" truth, that grace was "reigning through righteousness unto eternal life."

> 3] It is a gratifying proof of increasing light that so many modern expositors explain the words that follow ("and to all that are afar off") as referring to the Jews of the dispersion. To say that the promise was to Gentiles is utterly opposed to Scripture. (See e.g. Romans 9:4; 15:8; Ephesians 2:12; etc., etc.) It is certain, moreover, that not one of Peter's audience would put such a meaning on his words.

The covenants and promises to the Patriarchs neither exhausted nor limited the grace of God to men. And though "grace came by Jesus Christ," it was restrained during all His ministry on earth. "I have a baptism to be baptized with (He exclaimed), and how am I straitened till it be accomplished." Not till Divine righteousness was manifested in the death and resurrection of Christ, could Divine grace be fully and openly revealed. That there was forgiveness for the earnest seeker after God is not a distinctively Christian truth at all. It was always so. But the revelation of grace enthroned far transcends all that earlier ages knew. A parable may explain what that revelation means. "The Lord's day" [4] is one of our national institutions (for England is still a Christian country). And under English law that day is a day of grace, on which no court of justice can deal with criminals. Let their crimes be never so heinous, they cannot even be arraigned until the day of grace is over. And the present age is God's great day of grace; "He knoweth how… to reserve the unjust unto the day of judgment to be punished." (2 Peter 2:9)

> 4] Sunday is thus designated in our older statutes.

We have a Divine commentary upon this from the lips of Christ Himself, when, on that Sabbath day in the synagogue of Nazareth, He stood up to read the 61st chapter of Isaiah, and stopped in the middle of its opening sentence. The record tells us that having uttered the words "He sent me…to preach the acceptable year of the Lord," He closed the book and sat down. And then, in reply to the wondering looks of all the hearers, "He began to say unto them,

This day is this Scripture fulfilled in your ears." (Luke 4:16-21) "And the day of vengeance of our God" are the words that follow without break or pause, but He left those words unread. For till "the acceptable year of the Lord" has run its predestined course, the coming of "that great and terrible day of the Lord" is, through Divine longsuffering, delayed. In view of the rejection and death of the Son of God, the only possible alternatives were the doom of Sodom or the mercy of the gospel; and mercy triumphed.

The Indian Mutiny was followed by an amnesty. And so long as that amnesty remained in force, the honor of the Sovereign and Government of Britain was pledged to the rebels that on laying down their arms they would receive a pardon, instead of having their treasonable acts imputed to them. And during this day of grace, God is "not imputing unto men their trespasses." Nay, more than this - for Divine grace surpasses every human parallel - He is pleading with them to accept the gospel amnesty. These amazing truths are well-nigh unbelievable. And yet behind them lies another truth that is still more wonderful: the Divine prerogative of judgment has been delegated without reserve or limit to the Lord Jesus Christ; and He is now "exalted to be a Savior ."

And this is the solution of the crowning wonder of a silent heaven. God is silent because the gospel of His grace is His last word of mercy, and when again He breaks the silence it must be in wrath. The moral government of the world is not in abeyance, and men reap what they sow; but all direct punitive action against sin awaits the day of judgment. For in virtue of the Cross of Christ the throne of God has become a throne of grace. And the silence of heaven will be unbroken until the Lord Jesus passes to the throne of judgment.

In the ages before Christ came, men may well have craved for public proofs of the action of a personal God. But in the ministry and death and resurrection of the Lord Jesus Christ, God has so plainly manifested, not only His power, but His goodness and love-toward-man, that to grant evidential miracles, now, would be an acknowledgment that questions which have been for ever settled are still open. Moreover, miracles of another kind abound. For in recent years the gospel has achieved triumphs in heathendom, which transcend anything recorded in the Acts of the Apostles. And infidelity is thus confronted by surer proofs of the presence and power of God than any miracle in the natural sphere could offer. For miracles in the natural sphere are not necessarily a proof of Divine action they are the lure by which some of the demon cults of the present day ensnare their dupes; and the time may be near when such signs and wonders will abound.

While therefore we dare not limit what God may do in response to individual faith - for there is a gift of faith - to claim a sign is to tempt God, and to leave ourselves open to be deceived by the seducing spirits of these last days. [5]

> 5] These last clauses are taken from the Preface to the ninth edition of The Silence of God, a book in which I have sought to unfold the forgotten truth of "the mystery of God."

This truth of grace enthroned may be called the basal truth of the distinctively Christian revelation. And yet, in common with certain other truths of that revelation, it was lost in the post-apostolic age. The writings of the Patristic theologians will be searched in vain for a clear enunciation of it. And though it flashed out like April sunshine at the Reformation, it soon disappeared again. And, needless to say, the Romish system is a flagrant and open denial of it.

CHAPTER 5

THE MYSTERY OF CHRIST

THE Bible has suffered more from Christian exponents than from infidel assailants. The prophets of Israel, "moved by the Holy Spirit," spoke with united voice of a time when righteousness and peace would triumph and rule upon the earth; but "old-fashioned orthodoxy" interpreted their glowing periods much as an American crowd interprets the rhodomontade of political stump orators at election times! And thus the sublime words of the Hebrew Scriptures are supposed to find their fulfillment in the history of Christendom. They are read as referring to us and to our own age. And after us, the deluge! What wonder is it that sensible men of the world are skeptical both about the past predictions and the coming deluge! On this system of exegesis, for example, the sublime flights of Isaiah, when reduced to sober prose, find their realization - I repeat the phrase - in a pandemonium and a bonfire! This nightmare system of interpreting Holy Scripture makes the sacred pages seem to unbelief a hopeless maze of mysticism.

As we open the New Testament narrative we read that "In those days came John the Baptist, preaching in the wilderness of Judea, and saying, Repent, for the Kingdom of Heaven is at hand." And "when John was cast into prison," the Lord Himself took up this same testimony, "Repent, for the Kingdom of Heaven is at hand." (Matthew 3:1, 2; 4:17) Now the only meaning these words can bear, is that the time was at hand when heaven would rule upon earth, [1] a hope which, as the inspired Apostle declared at Pentecost, was the burden of Hebrew prophecy. But, as we have seen, the fulfillment of that hope has been postponed owing to the apostasy and sin of the Covenant people. And, because of its postponement, it has dropped out of the creed of Christendom; albeit Christendom, million-mouthed, daily recites the words the Lord Himself has given us with which to pray for its fulfillment - "Thy Kingdom come, Thy will be done on earth as it is done in heaven." With the vast majority of Christians that prayer is merely a pious incantation; but the words are His own, and they shall be realized to the full. And yet, "in our covert atheism" - to borrow a phrase from Charles Kingsley - those who cherish this belief are commonly regarded as fanatics.

> 1] For the only alternative would be that heaven was about to be brought under kingly rule. The word basileia means either kingly rule or the sphere in which that rule prevails.

Indeed the skeptical crusade which masquerades as "Higher Criticism" began with the assumption that God must be a cipher in the world which He Himself created; and so every book of Scripture which records any immediate Divine intervention in human affairs had to be got rid of. But the atheist, who is more intelligent and logical than these "Christian" pundits, triumphantly points to the absence of all such intervention as proof that there is no God at all And the majority even of real Christians are quite indifferent to the amazing mystery of a silent heaven. "The mystery of God" it is called in Scripture; and the time is foretold when "the mystery of God shall be finished." {Revelation 10:7) And, as the Seer declares, when that time comes, "great voices in heaven" will proclaim that "the sovereignty of this world is become the sovereignty of our Lord and of His Christ, and He shall reign." And God will then do that which the thoughtful wonder He does not do now and always, "He will give their reward to His servants and to His saints and to all that fear His name, and He will destroy them that destroy the earth." (Revelation 11:15-18) The first act in that awful judgment drama will include the doom of the professing Church on earth. (Revelation 19:2) And when a mighty voice proclaims that "God hath avenged the blood of His servants at her hand" - the unnumbered myriads of the martyrs - all heaven raises its hallelujah. And the Seer adds: "I heard as it were the voice of a great multitude, and as the voice of many waters, and as the voice of mighty thunderings, saying, Hallelujah, for the Lord God omnipotent reigneth." (Revelation 19:6)

But both the judgment of the Harlot and the restoration of the Covenant people await the close of the reign of grace. For, as we have seen, so long as grace is reigning, not only can there be no punitive action against human sin, but there can be no distinction made between one class of sinners and another. "There is no difference, for all have sinned": (Romans 3:22, 23) "There is no difference, for the same Lord is Lord of all, and is rich unto all that call upon Him." (Romans 10:12, 13) These are the principles of the reign of grace.

But did not the Lord Himself declare that "salvation is of the Jews"? And did He not say, "I am not sent but unto the lost sheep of the house of Israel"? How, then, can we reconcile statements so conflicting? This question has been already answered on a preceding page. Grace in its fullness is a "mystery" truth that could not be revealed until the Covenant people had lost their vantage-ground of privilege. But the same Scripture which records their "fall" declares with explicit definiteness that the economy resulting from that fall is abnormal and temporary; and that when the Divine purposes relating to this present age have been fulfilled, the covenant people shall be restored and "all Israel shall be saved." (Romans 11) [2]

> 2] Not "every Israelite," but Israel as a nation. For Romans 11. does not deal with questions of individual salvation at all, but with national and dispensational distinctions. (See Alford's Greek Testament Commentary.)

It is as clear as light, therefore, that this Christian dispensation differs as essentially from the future as it does from the past. I have sought to pillory the belief that earth is merely a recruiting-ground for heaven; but in a sense this characterizes the present age, marked, as it is, by failure and apostasy, and ending, as it will, in judgment. But it was not a forecast of "Christendom religion" that evoked the outburst of praise with which the dispensational chapters of Romans end. As the Apostle's spiritual vision became filled with the truth of a glorious heavenly purpose which God would accomplish in spite of sin and failure, he exclaimed, "O the depth of the riches both of the wisdom and knowledge of God! How unsearchable are His judgments, and His ways past finding out!"

And that purpose is revealed in "the mystery of Christ," which finds its fullest unfolding in the "Captivity Epistles" [3] - "the mystery which from all ages hath been hid in God" - namely, that sinners of earth are called to the highest glory of heaven in the closest possible relationship with Christ. The bridal relationship and glory of the heavenly election from the earthly people of the covenant might well seem the acme of everything to which redeemed humanity could ever rise; but this crowning "mystery" of the Christian revelation speaks of a bond more intimate and a glory more transcendent. The figure of the Bride betokens the closest union, but absolute oneness is implied in the figure of the Body.

>3] Ephesians and Colossians. It is not specifically mentioned in Philippians.

Some people regard the Old Testament as entirely superseded by the New, forgetting that all Scripture is God-breathed and profitable. And others again regard the New as merely an unfolding of the Old, forgetting that it reveals distinctively Christian truths of which no trace can be found in the Hebrew Scriptures. And in this category is "the mystery of Christ." The Apostle's words could not be more explicit: "By revelation He made known unto me the mystery which in other ages was not made known unto the sons of men." (Ephesians 3:3, 5)

This amazing climax of the New Testament revelation of grace is dragged into the mire by the Church of Rome, trading as it always does on the teaching of the Latin Fathers, who claimed for the professing Church all that pertains to the true and heavenly Church. The Body of Christ is a truth of practical import for the Christian, profoundly influencing his personal life on earth, and his relationships with his fellow Christians. But yet "the Church which is His body" is not on earth, nor can it have a corporate existence until all the members are brought in, and the Divine purpose respecting it is accomplished.

The parallel of the bridal relationship of the heavenly election out of Israel may teach us a lesson here. For it is not until the future age of the Apocalyptic visions that the Bride is displayed, and her marriage takes place. [4] In like manner the consummation and display of the Body relationship awaits the coming of the Lord. For in the Divine purpose it is entirely for the glory of our Lord and Savior that these elect companies of the redeemed are given positions of special nearness; and therefore the element of display has prominence.

4] See Note below.

NOTE CHAPTER 5: IS THE CHURCH THE BRIDE OF CHRIST?

"Is the Church the Bride of Christ?" Let us begin by correcting our terminology. In the Patmos visions we read of "the Bride, the Lamb's wife"; but "the Bride of Christ" is unknown to Scripture.

The first mention of the Bride is in John 3:29. In a Jewish marriage the "friend of the bridegroom "answered to our "groomsman." His most important duty was to present the bride to the bridegroom. And this was the place which the Baptist claimed. His mission was to prepare Israel to meet the Messiah, "to make ready a people prepared for the Lord" (Luke 1:17).

With the close of the Baptist's ministry, both the Bride and the Lamb disappear from the New Testament until we reach the Patmos visions. In Revelation 21 the Angel summons the Seer to behold "the Bride, the Lamb's wife"; and he showed him "the Holy Jerusalem descending out of heaven from God." The twelve gates of the city bear the names of the twelve tribes of the children of Israel, and in its twelve foundations are "the names of the twelve Apostles of the Lamb." And the foundations are "garnished with all manner of precious stones. For "it is the city that hath the foundations, whose builder and maker is God," (Hebrews 11:10) the city for which Abraham looked, when he turned his back upon the then metropolis of the world.

These Apostles of the Bride are not the Apostles who were given after the Ascension for the building up of the Body of Christ —

the Apostles of this Christian dispensation, chief among whom was Paul. They are the twelve Apostles of the Lord's earthly ministry to Israel, who shall sit on twelve thrones, judging the twelve tribes of Israel (Matthew 19:28). They are the Apostles of the Lamb. And "the Lord God Almighty and the Lamb" are the temple of this city; and the Lamb is the light thereof. Every part of the description and of the symbolism tends to make it clear that this city represents a relationship and a glory pertaining to the people of the covenant. And now we can understand why it is that it is called the Bride of the Lamb, and never the Bride of Christ. For, the mystery of the Body having now been revealed, Christ is identified with the Church which is His Body, whereas His relation to Israel is entirely *personal*.

What relation, then, does "Jerusalem which is above" bear to us? No need here for guessing, and no room for controversy, for on this point Scripture is explicit; "the Jerusalem that is above is free, which is our *Mother*" (Galatians 4:26, R.V.). We know that most of the Fathers were obsessed by the false belief that the Jew had been cast away for ever; but even this seems inadequate to account for their claiming the bridal relationship and glory for the Church of this dispensation.

There are two reasons for refusing to believe that the Church is the Bride. First, because Scripture nowhere states that it is the Bride, and secondly, because Scripture implicitly teaches that it is not the Bride. The question, Is A the wife of B? may be answered in the negative, either by pointing to C as his wife, or by indicating a relationship between A and B which is incompatible with that of marriage. And in both these ways Scripture vetoes the Church-Bride theory. For it teaches that the Bride is "our *Mother*," and that the Church is the Body of Christ.

The 5th chapter of Ephesians, moreover, ought to be accepted as making an end of controversy on this subject. The marriage relationship is there readjusted by a heavenly standard. If, therefore, the Church were the Bride, we should find it asserted here with emphatic prominence. But it is the Body relationship that is emphasized. Christ loved the Church, and the Church is His Body; therefore a

Christian is to love his wife as his own body. In the 81st verse the ordinance of Genesis 2:24 is re-enacted for the Christian with a new sanction and a new meaning. [1]

> 1] To interpret Ephesians 5:31 in a carnal sense is an outrage upon Scripture.

The "great mystery" of verse 32 is not that a man and his wife are one body, for such a use of the word "mystery" is foreign to Scripture. And moreover, the Apostle says expressly, "I am speaking about Christ and the Church." And the last verse of the chapter disposes of the whole question' "Nevertheless, though man and wife are not one body, yet because Christ and the Church are one body) let every one of you love his wife even as himself."

By a strange vagary of exegesis the Apostle's words in 2 Corinthians 11:2 are sometimes appealed to in support of the Church-Bride theory. Dr. Edersheim cites this passage to illustrate the position of groomsmen (or "friends of the bridegroom") at a Jewish marriage. Besides their other functions, they were, he says, "the guarantors of the bride's virgin chastity." [2] And the Apostle uses this figure to express his "jealousy" — his solicitude, for the Corinthian Christians.

> 2] Jewish Social Life, p. 153. It is noteworthy that in 2 Corinthians 11:2 the Apostle does not use the word "bride," but the ordinary word for an unmarried girl.

CHAPTER 6

THE LORD JESUS' RETURN

A FRUITFUL cause both of skepticism and of error is ignorance of what may be described as the ground plan and main purpose of the Old Testament Scriptures. "The whole Scriptures are a testimony to Christ: the whole history of the chosen people, with its types and its law and its prophecies, is a shewing forth of Him." [1] This, however, is the spiritual teaching of the Bible, which of course unspiritual men ignore, and I am here referring to what any intelligent reader ought to recognize. The book relates in the main to the Hebrew race. A brief preface of eleven chapters tells us all that we are concerned to know about "the earth and man," prior to the call of Abraham. We are there told of the creation and fall of Adam: that the human family sprang from a first man, but not as he came from the hand of God; for our first progenitor was a sinner and an outcast. In that same preface are briefly recorded certain great crises in human history, the most notable being the judgment of the flood. A new era was then inaugurated with the family of Noah. In course of time, however, abounding iniquity brought about another crisis, and God once more made a new beginning with a single family; though in fulfillment of His promise to Noah, He did not again destroy the guilty race.

> 1] These grand words are quoted from Dean Alford's commentary upon Luke 24:27.

With the call of Abraham begins the main narrative of the Bible, which relates solely to Abraham's descendants, other nations being mentioned only when, and so far as, Israel's interests became in some way identified with theirs. And from that time the continually swelling stream of Messianic promise and prophecy runs in the channel of the national history of Abraham's descendants. In our own days the spade of the explorer has brought to light abundant proofs that, at an earlier period, man had enjoyed a Divine revelation, and that he had utterly perverted and corrupted it. And now the revelation was entrusted to the Covenant people. They were chosen, so to speak, to be the Divine agents upon earth, and "unto them were committed the oracles of God."

Now in commerce an agent is appointed, not to restrict, but to facilitate, the supply of goods to the public; and also to ensure that they shall reach the public pure and unadulterated. And the Divine purpose in giving that position to the Covenant people, and "committing to them the oracles of God," was that the truth of God in its purity, and the blessings which accompany the knowledge of it, might be accessible to all mankind. We know what an employer would do if his agent acted as though the wares entrusted to him were his own, ignoring the interests of his principal, and treating the public with contempt. And this was precisely the case with Israel. The house of God, designed to be "a house of prayer for all nations," they treated as their own, and ended by making it "a den of thieves." And the Gentiles whom it was their duty to serve, they repelled with scorn.

This agency parable explains the Lord's words, "Salvation is of the Jews." "For Christ was a Minister of the circumcision for the truth of God"; (Romans 15:8) and during His ministry on earth He recognized the divinely accorded position of the Covenant people. But to resume my parable, if the principal dismisses his agent, he begins to deal directly with all who apply to him for supplies, and the dismissed agent must take his place as one of the public. And so was it with reference to Israel's "fall," "the setting-aside of them being the reconciling of the world." (Romans 11:15) Thus deprived of their stewardship, they are relegated to the position of other men. And the purpose and effect of their fall are stated in the words, "God hath concluded them all in unbelief that He might have mercy upon all." (Romans 11:32)

Thus it was that the way was opened up for the revelation of the great "mystery" truth of grace enthroned. For, as we have seen, that truth is absolutely incompatible with the recognition of special privileges, or of any vantage-ground of favor. Language could not be more explicit "All the world is brought under the judgment of God"; (Romans 3:19) There is no difference between the Jew and the Greek." (Romans 10:12) But the very same Scripture which teaches this declares with equal clearness and emphasis that "the gifts and calling of God are without repentance"; that "God has not cast away His people"; that "they are beloved for the fathers, sakes," and that they are yet to be restored to the favoured position which they have now lost through unbelief.

But Israel's restoration must involve as definite a change in God's dealings with the world as did that which marked the inauguration of the Christian dispensation. In fact that future dispensation must differ as essentially from the present, as the present differs from the past. For just as we aver that "God cannot lie," we may assert that He cannot act at the same time upon two wholly different and incompatible principles. Most certain it is, therefore, that some great crisis must occur in the spiritual sphere before the now pent-up stream of unfulfilled prophecy relating to Israel can again begin to flow. Does Holy Scripture foretell any crisis of the kind? Many students of prophecy believe that the Jews will regain possession of their land, and rebuild their temple, while still in unbelief. [2] And in view of recent events in the near East there is nothing improbable in such a forecast. The stage may be thus prepared for the great drama of the prophecies which await fulfillment. But the question here cannot be satisfied by proofs, however striking, of Jewish prosperity and influence on earth — events that might be due to advancing civilization and the exigencies of international politics. The solution of it must be sought for in Holy Scripture.

> 2] This would be merely a return to the state of things existing when Romans 11 was written.

The preceding pages have dealt with certain "mysteries" of the Christian revelation — truths which were kept secret until Apostolic times, and of which therefore no trace can be found in the Hebrew

Scriptures — the "mystery" of Israel's present rejection, and of the resulting economy on earth; the "mystery" of the Gospel; the "mystery of God," and the great "mystery of Christ." But there are also other "mysteries," and one of them seems to point to the very crisis about which we are seeking light. I refer to the neglected truth of the Coming of the Lord Jesus Christ to take His people home from earth to heaven. "For the Lord Himself shall descend from heaven with a shout, with the voice of the archangel, and with the trump of God; and the dead in Christ shall rise first; then we which are alive and remain, shall be caught up together with them in the clouds, to meet the Lord in the air; and so shall we ever be with the Lord." (1 Thessalonians 4:16, 17)

The Old Testament speaks plainly of His coming to bring deliverance to His earthly people upon the earth, after their restoration to Divine favor; and it contains many prophecies about His coming in judgment. These events, therefore, though specifically mentioned in the New Testament, are not "mystery" truths. But the language of Scripture is explicit respecting the event which will bring the present dispensation to a close. Here are the Apostle's words: Behold, I shew you a mystery; We shall not all sleep, but we shall all be changed, in a moment, in the twinkling of an eye, at the last trump for the trumpet shall sound, and the dead shall be raised incorruptible, and we shall be changed." (1 Corinthians 15:51, 52) [3] This "Coming" is sometimes called "the first stage of the Second Advent." But the phrase "Second Advent" has no Biblical sanction, (Hebrews 9:28) [4] it is the badge of the erroneous traditional belief that the Lord will never again appear until the last great judgment. Though the subject is one that calls for caution and reserve, we may assert with confidence that the numerous Scriptures which speak of the return of Christ cannot all refer to the same appearing.

> 3] See NOTE at the end of this chapter.

> 4] Hebrews 9:28 is misread when cited as a warrant for the phrase. The subject there is the doctrine of the Sin-offering. When Aaron passed within the veil, the people watched till he came out again to bless them. So also Christ, having been once offered to bear the sins of many, shall be seen a second time, apart from sin, by them that wait for Him unto salvation. The words of our A.V., "shall appear

the second time," convey a wrong impression. The word translated "appear" in both A. V. and R.V. is not that employed respecting the Lord's coming, but the ordinary word for being seen. I have therefore modified to this extent the R.V. reading given above.

This will have a literal fulfillment for Israel; but it is a great doctrinal truth for the people of God in every age. It is the Hebrews aspect of the truth of the Death and Resurrection of Christ in Romans.

Compare, for example, the "Coming" of the passages above cited from the Epistles, with that foretold by the heavenly messengers on the Mount of the Ascension. While the Lord was standing with His disciples on the Mount of Olives, "He was taken up, and a cloud received Him out of their sight." And as they were gazing heavenward "two men stood by them" and said, "This same Jesus who is taken up from you into heaven shall so come in like manner as ye have seen Him go into heaven." (Acts 1:11) "But surely," some one may exclaim, "this cannot mean that the Lord will ever again stand upon His feet on Mount Olivet" Yes, this is precisely what it means. The words are a confirmation of an Old Testament prophecy relating to times and events that are still future. In Zechariah 14:4 we read, "His feet shall stand in that day upon the Mount of Olives which is before Jerusalem upon the East." Now save that it is the same Christ in both cases, this "Coming" has nothing in common with that described in the Epistles. The one is strictly local, and it has to do with His earthly people in Jerusalem in the circumstances described by Zechariah; whereas the purpose of the other is to take out of the earth His people of "the heavenly calling," scattered the wide world over. And this will suffice to clear our minds of the error suggested by the phrase "the Second Advent," and thus to open the way for an unprejudiced inquiry as to the scope and meaning of the various Scriptures which speak of His coming again.

On such a subject, I repeat, caution and reserve should mark our thoughts and words; but on a few main points we may speak with definiteness and certainty. It is certain, for example, that before "the times of restitution of all things," the Lord will be manifested to put down all open evil and rebellion against God upon earth. Then again, the reign of righteousness and peace will last not less than a thousand years, [5] and not until after that period will be His appearing for the last great judgment. The question arises then, whether the "Coming" described in 1 Corinthians and 1 Thessalonians is connected with any of these "Appearings." And here a brief pause for "stock-taking" may expedite the inquiry. We have seen that the Covenant people, though now set aside, are to be again restored to Divine favor, and that "the receiving of them" necessarily implies what is called "a change of dispensation." And we have seen also that "the times of restitution of all things" fall within that future dispensation. Now this obviously creates a presumption that there will be a "Coming" to bring this "Christian dispensation" of ours to an end. It remains to be seen then whether such a presumption is confirmed or vetoed by Scripture. And here, as in the preceding chapters, the appeal shall be neither to authority, nor to prejudice, but only to Holy Scripture itself, and to the intelligence of the reader.

> 5] The "thousand years" of Revelation 20:4 is taken by some to mean, not a definite chronological era, but a vast period of time.

But let us not forget the momentous importance of the issue, for it must decide for us whether the Lord's return is a present hope, or merely an event in the great drama of prophecy to be fulfilled at some future time, when most, if not all, of us shall have finished our course on earth. And this suggests another thought. If such a hope be a mere delusion, it is a delusion which is full of comfort, and has a sanctifying influence upon the life. Why, then, it may well be asked, should any Christian wish to rob us of it? And yet the belief is attacked with untiring zeal, and at times with acrimony, as though it ranked with heresies that dishonour Christ. It is specially to the ephemeral literature on the subject that this reproach attaches; a literature that is generally marked by confusion of thought and neglect of the main landmarks that guide the intelligent interpretation of Scripture. The following, for example, is a typical sentence: "The Lord Jesus Himself warned His disciples against the thought of an immediate coming, and sketched a whole series of events which should happen before His personal return, adding, For all these things must come to pass, but the end is not yet.' — Matthew 24:6."

Some of us have learned to distinguish between "the coming of the Son of Man" in judgment, "to gather out of His Kingdom all things that offend and them which do iniquity," and the coming of the Lord, as Savior, to call His people out of earth to heaven. (Matthew 13:41) [6]

> 6] The 40th and 41st verses of ch. 24 are explained by verse 31. It is not taking His elect out of the earth, but gathering them together upon earth for the earthly kingdom.

In the very same discourse in which the Lord gave the warning above quoted, He gave another warning still more emphatic and explicit. Here are His words "Watch therefore for ye know not what hour your Lord doth come"; and again, "Watch therefore, for ye know neither the day nor the hour wherein the Son of Man cometh." (Matthew 24:42; 25:13) But as the one warning seems to support the writer's argument, whereas the other entirely refutes it, the one is quoted and the other is ignored. Indeed the system followed by writers of this school is to separate texts from their context, and throwing them into hotchpotch, to pick out any that suit their purpose. And it is not open to them to plead that this particular advent is not the same as that described in the Epistles. For their argument depends on the assumption, thus proved to be false, that there cannot be an unheralded advent of Christ; and in view of this Scripture, that argument collapses like a child's house of cards.

This hotchpotch system of exegesis makes it easy to prove or disprove almost anything. And it leaves the Bible open to infidel attacks; for if it be discredited by contradictions, it cannot be Divine, or even true. But the intelligent Bible student has the clew to the seeming labyrinth. What is needed, as Lord Bacon quaintly puts it, is "that every prophecy of Scripture be sorted with the event fulfilling the same." The task of attempting some "sorting" of this kind is reserved for another chapter.

NOTE CHAPTER 6: THE LORD'S COMING IN GREEK WORD

THERE are three different words used in the Greek Testament in relation to the Lord's Coming.

Parousia means primarily "presence" (see 2 Corinthians 10:10; Philippians 2:12), and it is used of any person's arrival (see, e.g., 1 Corinthians 16:17; 2 Corinthians 7:6, 7; etc.). In secular use it applied specially to any state visit. In the following passages it is used of the return of Christ: Matthew 24:3, 27, 37, 39; 1 Corinthians 15:23; 1 Thessalonians 2:19; 3:13; 4:15; 5:23; 2 Thessalonians 2:1, 8; James 5:7, 8; 2 Peter 1:16; 1 John 2:28.

Apokalupsis ("revelation" or "manifestation") is used of the Advent in 1 Corinthians 1:7; 2 Thessalonians 1:7; 1 Peter 1:7, 13.

Epiphaneia ("appearing") occurs in 2 Thessalonians 2:8 (brightness); 1 Timothy 6:14; 2 Timothy 1:10; 4:1, 8; Titus 2:13.

And the verb *phaneroo* ("to appear or be manifested") is used in Colossians 3:4; 1 Peter 5:4; 1 John 2:28; 3:2.

The attempt has been made to apportion these words to the several future manifestations of the Lord Jesus Christ. A reference to the passages where they occur will enable the Bible student to judge whether this distinction can be sustained; or whether the words do not rather indicate different phases or aspects of the various "Comings" foretold in Scripture.

CHAPTER 7

THE GENTILE CHURCH

ON the subject of the Coming of the Lord the First Epistle to the Thessalonians has an altogether exceptional importance. And the more closely we study the condition and circumstances of those to whom it was addressed, our sense of its importance will increase.

The opening clauses of the 17th chapter of the Acts contain all that the narrative records about the Apostle's ministry in Thessalonica. And were it not for the incidental reference of verse 11, we might suppose that his preaching in the synagogue was crowned with unusual success; whereas that verse tells us that the Jews refused even to consider the Scriptures on which his appeals to them were based. We may therefore assume with confidence that, after his three Sabbath days' "reasoning" with them, the Apostle "turned to the Gentiles," and that the 4th verse of the chapter gives the results, not of his synagogue ministry, but of all his evangelistic labors in Thessalonica.

We thus learn that some of the Jews believed, "and of the devout Greeks a great multitude." It is often assumed that these Greeks were proselytes, albeit it is most improbable that the whole company of the proselytes connected with the synagogue were numerous enough to justify the phrase "a great multitude." But the question is absolutely settled by the Apostle's explicit statement that these converts had been pagan idolaters. (1 Thessalonians 1:9) And as his Epistle makes no reference to Hebrew Christians, we may assume that the "some among the Jews" who believed must have been few in number. It is certain that the Church of the Thessalonians was essentially Gentile. And the bearing of this fact will appear in the sequel.

How long the Apostle remained among them is a matter of conjecture; but the facts give proof that his sojourn cannot have been brief. For it is quite incredible that a congregation of recently converted pagans, if left to themselves, would have reached and maintained such a standard of saintship as to become a pattern church, exerting an influence "not only in Macedonia and Achaia, but in every place." (1 Thessalonians 1:8) Results like these must have been the fruit of much doctrinal teaching and not a little pastoral care. And that they enjoyed such a ministry is definitely indicated by the many references to it scattered throughout both Epistles. But at last a storm of persecution robbed them of the Apostle's presence. After a brief but happy ministry in Berea he was again obliged to flee, and he journeyed to Athens. During his stay in Athens some grave tidings reached him about the Thessalonian converts, tidings which raised fears whether all his labors among them had not been in vain. (1 Thessalonians 3:1-5) And much though he needed companionship and help at such a time, he commissioned Timothy to return at once to Macedonia. He himself passed on to Corinth, where in due course Timothy rejoined him, bringing him the particulars he longed for about the trouble in the Thessalonian Church. And the nature of that trouble is clearly indicated by the letter which he forthwith addressed to them. It was due to no lapse toward either immorality or heresy, but to the fact that certain of their leaders had been martyred. (1 Thessalonians 2:14, 15; 3:4) [1] We fail to appreciate the fears and difficulties of these Gentile converts of early days. The faith of the spiritual Christian who has the Bible in his hands, and to whom the story of the Church's sufferings is an open page, may pierce the darkest clouds; but these Thessalonians had no such glorious records of a faith-tried past, and it is doubtful to what extent they had access even to the Hebrew Scriptures. They had been told, moreover, that He in whom they believed had all power in heaven and earth; and yet they had been left a prey to the hate of their heathen enemies. But with exquisite tenderness the Apostle reminds them that they were not only the followers of the Hebrew

Christians who had endured similar sufferings from their fellow-Jews, but also the disciples of the Lord Jesus, who had Himself been put to death by them.

> 1] That it was the leaders who had fallen is an obvious inference: it is so in every persecution.

The groundwork of the Epistle was evidently supplied by the tidings which Timothy had brought him. [2] But the Epistle was (to change the figure) a casket to convey to them a special message which the Lord had entrusted to him, a message to comfort their hearts and confirm their faith. That this was its character is plainly indicated by the words "This we are saying unto you in the word of the Lord." We cannot solve the mysteries of inspiration, but from certain passages in his Epistles it is clear that special revelations were occasionally received by the Apostle Paul with peculiar definiteness. By a revelation of this kind, and at this very time, he had "received" the very words in which to preach the Gospel in Corinth. After the utter failure of his testimony at Athens, we can well believe that, with importunate supplication, he may have pleaded for special guidance in preaching to the Corinthians. And he reminds them of this in his First Epistle, in restating the Gospel he had proclaimed to them. For here the Revised Version of 1 Corinthians 15:2 is explicit' "I make known, I say, in what words I preached it unto you; for I delivered unto you first of all that which I also received" — the identical phrase he uses in the 11th chapter with reference to the revelation accorded him respecting the Lord's Supper.

> 2] This appears very plainly from the first part of both ch. 4 and ch. 5.

Here, then, are the words in which he conveyed the Lord's special message to the Thessalonians" (13) But we would not have you to be ignorant, brethren, concerning the sleeping ones, that ye may not sorrow, even as the rest do who have no hope. (14) For if we believe that Jesus died and rose again, even so them also who fell asleep through Jesus will God bring together with Him. (15) For this we say unto you in the word of the Lord, that we who are living, who remain behind unto the coming of the Lord, shall in no wise gain an advantage over them who fell asleep, (16) because the Lord Himself shall come down from heaven with a shout, with the voice of the archangel and with the trumpet of God: and the dead in Christ shall rise first: [3] (17) then we who are living who remain behind, shall be caught up all together with them, in the clouds, to meet the Lord, into the air: and so shall we be always with the Lord. (18) So then comfort one another with these words" (1 Thessalonians 4:13-18).

> 3] Alford's note here is: "This first has no reference whatever to the 'first resurrection' (Revelation 20:5, 6), but answers to then in verse 17." This is of great importance if we are to understand Scripture aright. The first resurrection of Revelation 20 is so called in relation to the resurrection after the 1000 years. It belongs to the future dispensation of a restored Israel. The faithful martyrs of the Great Tribulation will then be raised from the dead. (New Testament Commentary, in loco.)

This is Dean Alford's translation of the passage, save only that in verse 18 his version reads, "them that are sleeping." The more literal rendering, "the sleeping ones," makes it still clearer that, whereas the 16th verse speaks of all the dead in Christ, the reference in the preceding verses is to the particular individuals whose loss the Thessalonians were mourning. The popular rendering of the 14th verse, "them that sleep in Jesus," is an obvious mis-translation. And a more literal rendering even than Alford's would bring out more fully the exquisite pathos of the Lord's message to them. For the primary meaning of the verb koimao is not to fall asleep but to put to sleep. What troubled these sorely-tried disciples was that they regarded the death of their friends as a sign that the Lord had failed them. And this is the Lord's answer. As it was for His own name's sake that they had suffered, He speaks of them as having been put to sleep by Himself. It is as though He said, "Though I was the cause of their death, I have not failed them. Was not I Myself put to death? And as surely as I died and rose again, they too shall rise, and God will bring them with Me at My coming." And our sense of the infinite grace of this is intensified by the fact that the message of hope and comfort is given in the name of His humiliation — the name under which He Himself was slain! It is His first recorded message to His saints on earth after His ascension. And in that same name is His final message, given us upon the last page of Holy Scripture' "I, Jesus...am the bright and morning star...Surely I am coming quickly."

But what voice has this message for ourselves today? This is the question which specially concerns us. And to enable us to answer it, we do well to consider what it meant, and what it was intended to mean, for those to whom it was primarily addressed hence the importance of this inquiry respecting the condition and circumstances of the Thessalonian Christians. Let us keep clearly in view that they were Gentile converts. They had no share, therefore, in Israel's national hopes; nor do the Epistles give us any reason to believe that they had any doctrinal knowledge of those hopes. The Pentecostal promise which, as a present hope, the Jews had already forfeited, was that, in fulfillment of Hebrew prophecy, Christ would come to His earthly people to put all things right upon the earth. And the literal definiteness of that hope appears from the promise of the Ascension day, confirming Zechariah's explicit words. (Acts 1:11; Zechariah 14:4) But these Thessalonians had "turned to God from idols...to wait for His Son from heaven." And the Lord's message to them plainly indicates the meaning of that special hope of theirs. Now if His coming to call away His heavenly people signifies the same thing as His coming to deliver Jerusalem and the Jews from Gentile armies, we must conclude that in Scripture words may mean anything, and all discussion of them is idle.

It may be said perhaps that although the earthly hope and the heavenly hope differ so essentially, they will be fulfilled at the same advent. But any presumption there may be in favor of this view rests entirely on popular misbeliefs about "the Second Advent." There is no proof whatever of it, and it clashes with the teaching of the Epistles. The Thessalonians were waiting for the Lord. But, for some reason unknown to us, they believed that at His coming it was only the living who would be called away. The martyred dead therefore had lost their part in this "blessed hope," and as their "call" would thus be deferred till a resurrection in the distant future, their death was mourned with a hopeless sorrow.

Now if our popular misbeliefs were true, the Apostle would surely have told them that their grief was due to the error of expecting the speedy return of Christ they had mistaken a future for a present hope, and before the Advent could take place they would all have joined their martyred friends "beyond the veil." But in striking contrast with this, mark the God-given words of the Epistle, "that we who are living, who remain behind unto the coming of the Lord, shall in no wise gain an advantage over the sleeping ones." "WE who are living": if they were wrong in believing that the Lord might come in their own lifetime, could even a trained lawyer have drafted words better fitted to confirm them in the error!

I repeat, therefore, with increased emphasis, that the knowledge which the Thessalonian Epistle gives us of the circumstances of those to whom it was written, and of their special griefs and difficulties, lends to its teaching a peculiar definiteness and importance. Indeed if our expectation of the Lord's return had no other Scriptural warrant, this Epistle might suffice us. But the references to the hope are many in other Epistles also. To deal with them in full detail, however, would be foreign to the scheme of these pages, and a few leading passages will here suffice.

The 15th chapter of 1 Corinthians claims very special notice. That wonderful exposition and defense of the great truth of the resurrection leads up to the following pregnant words: —

> "Behold, I shew you a mystery; We shall not all sleep, but we shah all be changed, in a moment, in the twinkling of an eye, at the last trump: for the trumpet shall sound, and the dead shall be raised incorruptible, and we shah be changed. For this corruptible must put on incorruption, and this mortal must put on immortality. So when this corruptible shall have put on incorruption, and this mortal shall have put on immortality, then shall be brought to pass the saying that is written, Death is swallowed up in victory. Oh death, where is thy sting? Oh grave, where is thy victory? The sting of death is sin; and the strength of sin is the law. But thanks be to God, which giveth us the victory through our Lord Jesus Christ. Therefore, my beloved brethren, be ye steadfast, unmovable, always abounding in the work of the Lord, foras-

much as ye know that your labor is not in vain in the Lord." (1 Corinthians 15:51-58)

"We shall not all sleep" Is this to be read as a mere recital of the obvious fact that when the Lord returns He will find some of His people living upon earth? What an empty platitude to introduce into one of the sublimest passages in all the New Testament Epistles! The purpose of the words is clear. The Corinthians were "waiting for the coming of the Lord Jesus Christ"; (1 Corinthians 1:7) and he thus seeks to confirm them in that attitude, and (as the 58th verse so clearly indicates) to make it increasingly a present hope, fitted to influence heart and life. Therefore is it that, though he speaks of the dead in the third person, he always speaks of the living in the first — "We shall not all sleep." For while the Resurrection is the hope of those who fall asleep, the Coming is the hope of living saints. But if he had known that the advent was an event in a remote future, this would have been so misleading that in a merely human writing it would be regarded as almost a *suggestio falsi*!

A like thought is suggested by his reference to this truth in his Second Epistle. The symbolism of the 5th chapter is as simple as it is graphic. Our "natural body" is likened to a tent, the spiritual body to a house. Not a house like the Jerusalem temple, built on earth by human hands, and liable to perish; but a building of God, eternal, and in the heavens. Then the symbolism assumes another phase. Death is likened to our being unclothed; and in contrast with being thus stripped naked, our receiving the heavenly body without passing through death is symbolized by our being "clothed upon." Three distinct conditions are thus indicated — clothed, clothed upon, and found naked. The first is our condition during our life on earth, and the last is that to which death reduces us. This is plain to all; but the "being clothed upon" is apt to be misunderstood. It does not refer to the Resurrection, but to the change which the Coming of the Lord will bring to those "who are alive and remain." [4]

> 4] "Being found naked" is the condition produced by death. "Being clothed upon" refers, not to the Resurrection but to the coming of the Lord. "The thought is that of one who... wishes, as he expects, to remain till that Coming (comp. 1 Corinthians 15:51; 1 Thessalonians 4:15), to let the incorruptible body supervene on the corruptible,

to be changed instead of dying." (Bishop Ellicott's *New Testament Commentary for English Reader's*.)

Death is an outrage upon life, a hideous and hateful outrage. And yet (as the Apostle wrote to the Philippians)"to have died is gain"; [5] for at death do we not pass from earth to be "with Christ," which is "far better"? So here he says, We are "willing rather" to be absent from the body and to be "at home with the Lord." "Willing rather" denotes a bare preference; but when he speaks of the hope to be realized at the Coming, "earnestly desiring" is the phrase he uses. And his purpose in all this, as the sequel plainly shows, is not to instruct them in eschatology, but to enforce the practical bearing of the hope upon life and conduct. How unreasonable this would be, if the Coming were not a present hope!

> 5] "To die is gain" is the evil creed of a suicide. The Apostle never said that!"

The closing sentence of the 3rd chapter of Philippians is of special interest in this connection' "Our citizenship is in heaven; from whence also we wait for a Savior, the Lord Jesus Christ; who shall fashion anew the body of our humiliation, that it may be conformed to the body of His glory, according to the working whereby He is able even to subject all things unto Himself." (Philippians 3:20, 21, R.V.) Here again, mark the form of the sentence — the present tense, and the first person plural — "We are expecting a Savior." But this is not all. When challenged by the question, "How are the dead raised up and With what body do they come!" the Apostle's answer was, "Thou fool!" But when in that same chapter he came to speak of the living, his words were explicit, "We shall all be changed." And here to the Philippians he uses a kindred, but still stronger word — the body of our humiliation shah be transformed. The holy dead, it need not be said, will be raised in bodies like the Lord's. But it is not of the Resurrection that he is speaking here, nor yet of the buried dust of them that are "fallen asleep," but of the "flesh and blood" of the living men whom he is addressing; and to them he says, "We are waiting for the Savior who will transform the body of our humiliation."

First Corinthians was one of the Apostle's earlier Epistles' Philippians was written toward the close of his life, and after the close of his special ministry to Israel. But the doctrine of the Coming is unchanged — the hope is the same; the only difference being that, when writing from his Roman prison, he uses a stronger word than ever before — "We are assiduously and patiently waiting for the Savior." [6] And still further to impress upon the Philippian saints the reality and definiteness of that hope, he adds, "The Lord is at hand." [7] The Apostle's words to Titus may fittingly conclude this notice of his teaching about the Coming of the Lord. In this Epistle, believed to have been written in the very year of his martyrdom, we find the same glad note of comfort and hope. "For the grace of God hath appeared, salvation-bringing to all men, disciplining us in order that, denying ungodliness and worldly lusts, we should live soberly, justly and godly in this present world, looking for that blessed hope, even the glorious appearing of our great God and Savior Jesus Christ." (Titus 2:11-13) [8]

> 6] This is the meaning given to the word in Grimm's Lexicon.. It occurs also in Romans 8:19, 23, 25; 1 Corinthians 1:7; Galatians 5:5; Hebrews 9:28. Grimm remarks that it is scarcely found out of the New Testament.
>
> 7] The 14th verse of Philippians 3 is sometimes taken as referring to the Coming. But verse 12 vetoes such an exegesis. See NOTE at the end of this chapter. 8 "Bringing salvation to all men" suggests a serious error; and moreover the word here used is an adjective. And surely, having regard to English idiom, the A. V. Hendiadys rendering, "the glorious appearing," is right, for The R.V. rendering throws a wholly false emphasis upon "glory." It is a strange exegesis which makes "the great God" a synonym for The Father: Scripture does not employ one term when another is intended.

Will any one dare to rob us of these words by referring them to "the great and terrible day of the Lord". True it is that the Lord Jesus shall be "revealed in flaming fire to take vengeance on them that know not God." But to call that a "blessed hope" would savor of the spirit of the Spanish Inquisition, rather than of the Christian's grace-taught heart! One word more. In common with certain other distinctive truths of the Christian revelation, this of the Coming has peculiar prominence in the Epistles of the Apostle Paul. But in proof that it was a hope shared by "all saints" in the Apostolic age, appeal may be made to the following words of the Apostle Peter "Knowing that I must shortly put off this tabernacle, even as our Lord Jesus Christ hath shewed me." (2 Peter 1:14) *Me* emphatic. And the student of evidence will ask what need there could have been for such a special revelation to Peter, if death were the common lot of all; for when these words were written he must have been nearing his three-score years and ten.

NOTE CHAPTER 7: PHILIPPIANS 3:8-14 [1]

1] Referring to the exegesis of Philippians 3:8-14, my greatly esteemed friend, the late Dr. E. W. Bullinger, added the following note to a most cordial commendation of, Forgotten Truths:

"We would remind our readers that ano in Philippians 3:14 is not an adjective, meaning 'high' as to quality, but an adverb, meaning 'upward' as to direction; and that the verb katantao (Philippians 3:11)…is always used of a personal or material arrival at a definite situation." This is an enigma to me. Of the thirteen occurrences of katantao, nine are found in Acts and four in the Epistles (1 Corinthians 10:11; 14:36; Ephesians 4:13; and Philippians 3:11). Save only in Acts 26:7, where he quotes the Apostle Paul, the Evangelist always uses the word in its primary meaning of "a personal or material arrival at a given situation." But the word has a secondary meaning, which Grimm defines as "to attain to a thing"; and Philippians 3:11 is one of the passages he cites to illustrate this. Indeed a careful study of the texts above enumerated suggests that the Apostle Paul uses the word always and only in this secondary sense.

And as for ano, the exposition here given of "the high calling of God" is wholly unaffected by the fact that the word is an adverb. I would maintain that in Philippians 3:14 it means neither "high as to quality," nor yet "upward as to direction," but is used (as in Colossians 3:1 and 2) to express the "heavenly" origin and character of the "calling." In keeping with this, Grimm's Lexicon explains Philippians 3:14 as "the calling made in heaven."

If the commonly received exegesis of Philippians 3:8-14 be correct, we are faced by the astounding fact that the author of the Epistle to the Romans and of the 15th chapter of 1 Corinthians — the Apostle who was in a peculiar sense entrusted with the supreme revelation of grace — announced when nearing the close of his ministry that the resurrection was not, as he had been used to teach, a blessing which Divine grace assured to all believers in Christ, but a prize to be won by the sustained efforts of a life of wholly exceptional saintship.

Nor is this all. In the same Epistle he has already said, "To me to live is Christ, and to have died is gain"; whereas, *ex hypothesi*, it now appears that his chief aim in life was to earn a right to the resurrection; and that death, instead of bringing gain, would have cut him off before he had reached the standard of saintship needed to secure that prize! For his words are explicit, "not as though I had already attained."

Here was one who was "not a whit behind the chiefest Apostles"; who excelled them all in labors and sufferings for his Lord, and in the "visions and revelations" accorded to him; whose prolonged ministry, moreover, was accredited by "mighty signs and wonders by the power of the Spirit of God." And yet, "being now such an one as Paul the aged," he was in doubt whether he should have part in that resurrection which he had taught all his pagan Corinthian converts to hope for: for to them it was he wrote the words, "we shall *all* be changed."

Such is the exposition of the Apostle's teaching in many a standard commentary. And yet the passage which is thus perverted reaches its climax in the words, "Our citizenship is in heaven, from whence we are looking for the Savior , the Lord Jesus Christ, who shall fashion anew the body of our humiliation that it may be conformed to the body of His glory."

"Our citizenship is in heaven " here is the clew to the teaching of the whole passage. The truth to which his words refer is more clearly stated in Ephesians 2:6 - God has "quickened us together with Christ, and raised us up with Him, and made us sit with Him in the heavenly places in Christ." More clearly still is it given in Colossians 3:1-3: "If then ye were raised together with Christ, seek the things that are above, where Christ is seated on the right hand of God. Set your mind on the things that are above, not on the things that are on earth. For ye died, and your life is hid with Christ in God."

Ephesians and Colossians, be it remembered, were written at the same period of his ministry as Philippians; and in the light of these Scriptures we can read this chapter aright. To "win Christ" (ver. 8), or to apprehend, or lay hold of, that for which he had been laid hold of, or apprehended (ver. 12); or in other words, to realize practically in his life on earth what was true of him doctrinally as to his standing before God in heaven — this is what he was reaching toward, and what, he says, he had not "already attained."

The "high calling" of ver. 14 is interpreted by some to mean Christ's calling up His own to meet Him in the air (a blessing assured to all "who are alive and remain unto the Coming of the Lord"); but this is not in keeping with the plain words — God's high calling in Christ Jesus, i.e. what God has called us (made us) to be in Christ.

If this passage refers to the literal resurrection, then the words "not as though I had already attained must mean that, while here on earth, and before the Lord's Coming, the Apostle hoped either to undergo the change of ver. 21, or else to win some sort of saintship diploma, or certificate, to ensure his being raised at the Coming. These alternatives are inexorable; and they only need to be stated to ensure their rejection.

One word more. If the Apostle Paul, after such a life of saintship and service, was in doubt as to his part in the resurrection, no one of us, unless he be the proudest of Pharisees or the blindest of fools, will dream of attaining it. In fact we shall dismiss the subject from our minds.

CHAPTER 8

THE SECOND COMING, WHEN?

IT is a fact of great significance that the Coming of the Lord is never mentioned in the Epistles of the New Testament save in an incidental manner - never once as a doctrine that needed to be expounded, but only and always as a truth with which every Christian was supposed to be familiar.

This is strikingly exemplified by the passages already cited. And it explains what to some may seem strange, that there is no notice of the Coming in Ephesians or Colossians. If these were the latest of the Apostle Paul's Epistles, the omission might possibly suggest to some that the hope had been abandoned. But not only does it appear in Philippians, which was also written from his Roman prison; but, as we have seen, one of the fullest and clearest references to it is contained in Titus, which was written at a still later date than "the Captivity Epistles." The Coming is not mentioned in Ephesians and Colossians; but neither is justification by faith. A "Higher Critic" might find in this a proof of different authorship. And a lawyer might think that each book of the New Testament ought to begin with recitals, and with many a "whereas," referring to the contents of earlier writings; but happily the Scriptures are not written in that fashion The fact is clear then, that in Apostolic times the converts were taught to expect the Lord's return. So certain is this indeed, that discussion would be useless with any who deny it. [1] But what explanation can be found for the no less salient fact that, although we have reached the twentieth century of the Christian era, the hope appears to be no nearer its fulfillment? Rejecting the infidel taunt that the teaching was erroneous, and the hope which it inspired a delusion, we are shut up to choose between the following alternatives. Either the promise has been cancelled or withdrawn; or else, owing to some cause which came fully into operation after the close of the sacred Canon, its fulfillment has been delayed. But all the promises of God are assured in Christ, (2 Corinthians 1:20) and there is no variableness with Him. The one alternative, therefore, we reject: the other shall be considered in the sequel.

> 1] I say this because the fact is admitted by expositors of various schools, many of whom have no sympathy with the hope.

Some indeed would seek to escape from this conclusion by a mistaken reading of First Thessalonians. They take the day of the Lord in chapter 5 to be a synonym for the Coming of the Lord in chapter 4; and they appeal to the Second Epistle in proof that notable events must precede its happening. Even if this were tenable, it would have no bearing upon the Epistles to the other Churches, And that it is quite untenable appears from the fact that the Coming of the Lord is a distinct event, whereas the day of the Lord is an era, the course and character of which are described both by the Hebrew prophets, and by the Lord Himself in the "Second Sermon on the Mount." (Matthew 24)

But it may be asked, Does not that sermon definitely declare that the Lord will come at the close of "the great tribulation"? Yes, truly; but the seeming relevance of this to the present question depends entirely on the prevalent error respecting "the Second Advent." The promise of the Incarnation was so utterly incredible that it may well have staggered faith. But now that He has lived upon earth and gone back to heaven, His coming again seems a natural sequence to His ascension. Indeed if we were left to reason out the matter, we should expect Him to return again and again. And this is precisely what Scripture tells us to look for. Common sense might veto the suggestion that His coming as Avenger and Judge is the event described as "that blessed hope." And it is no less clear that the message received by the disciples on the Mount of the Ascension does not relate to the same Coming as the Apostle's words to the Thessalonians and the Corinthians. But the Coming of the Lord as Savior is now confounded with "the day of the Lord" - the day of wrath. In fact the error which the Second Epistle to the Thessalonians was designed to correct is now in the creed of Christendom!

Are we to believe that the Gentile converts were taught to live in expectation of the Coming, although, *ex hypothesi*, before that hope could be realized the people of God were doomed to pass through a time of horror unparalleled in all the ages? And yet no Epistle except that to the Thessalonians contained a warning word about that awful time. And the Apostle's words to them, if intended as a warning, could scarcely have been more deceptive. For after speaking of the Coming as a present hope with which to comfort one another, he went on to speak of the day of the Lord as pertaining to the "times and seasons" of Israel's national history. To the world that day would come as a day of wrath, for, "when they shall say peace and safety, then sudden destruction cometh upon them." But in contrast with this, the Apostle adds, "God has not appointed us to wrath, but to obtain deliverance by our Lord Jesus Christ." What meaning could the Thessalonians put upon these words, save that the appointed deliverance was by the Coming of the Lord? And to make this still more clear he again exhorts them to comfort one another with his words. "Times and seasons" these well-known words come from the Book of Daniel. The Lord made use of them when, on the Mount of the Ascension, the disciples asked Him, "Wilt Thou at this time restore the kingdom to Israel?" "It is not for you (He said) to know times or seasons." And this reply confirmed the truth that underlay the question. The word which He had spoken by the mouth of Daniel shall be fulfilled, and the Kingdom shall yet be restored to Israel; but "the times and seasons" are with God.

I will offer no conjectures as to what the course of events would have been if the nation had accepted the Divine amnesty proclaimed at Pentecost. Certain it is, however, that none of the words of Christ will fail of their ultimate fulfillment on account of Israel's rejection of the proffered mercy But so long as Israel's national position is in abeyance, the stream of fulfillment is tided back; or to change the figure, the hands upon the dial of prophetic time are motionless. Without this clew to guide us in our study of them, the Scriptures appear to be full of confusion, if not of error. "The times and seasons" rest with Him to whom a thousand years are as one day. And when in Matthew 24, for example, the Lord addressed His hearers as though they themselves would pass through the Great Tribulation, we recognize that this would have proved literally true if the Jews had accepted Him as their Messiah. But with Romans 11 before us, we recognize also that, when Israel was cast aside the clock of prophetic time was stopped, to be set in motion once again at the close of this intercalary "Christian dispensation." And then the Lord's prophetic words shall be fulfilled as though this age of ours had never intervened.

And now, if we will but rise above the mists of controversy, and arguments based on isolated texts, and take note of the prominent landmarks of prophetic interpretation, and the distinctive truths of the Christian revelation, we shall find abundant proof that the fulfillment of Matthew 24. belongs to a future age, and to an economy essentially different from our own.

The last verse of Daniel 9 might almost be paraphrased in the language of modern diplomacy. The "prince" of that prophecy - the last great Kaiser of Christendom - will make a seven years' treaty with the Jews, guaranteeing respect for the ordinances of their religion. But in the middle of that term he will violate the treaty, and defile the Temple by enthroning himself within it. This last particular we learn from 2 Thessalonians 2:4. And the Lord's own words, spoken with express reference to this very prophecy, for the guidance of His Jewish people who will witness its fulfillment, warn them that the defilement of the holy place is to be the signal for immediate flight; "for then shall be great tribulation such as never was since the beginning of the world." (Matthew 24:21) Daniel's prophecy, to which the Lord explicitly refers, describes it as "a time of trouble such as never was since there was a nation," (Daniel 12:1) and other references to it might be quoted from the Hebrew prophets, such for example as the words of Jeremiah, who calls it "the time of Jacob's trouble." (Jeremiah 30:7)

Here is something to disturb the complacency of Christians who are in the habit of treating the Bible as though it were a lottery bag of texts, rejecting what they slightingly call "dispensationalism."

The Apocalyptic visions indicate that Christendom will come within the awful persecution of the latter days, whereas these Old Testament prophecies relate only to Judah and Jerusalem, and in the Lord's own teaching there is never a word to suggest that they will have any wider range. How is this to be explained? Not by saying, with the Higher Critics, that the Lord was ignorant, but by recognizing that this "Christian Dispensation" is a New Testament "mystery," unknown to the people of God, and unnoticed in the Word of God, until after Israel had been set aside, and the Apostle to the Gentiles had received his call. Therefore was it that, from the standpoint of the Mount of Olives, the world consisted of Israel and heathendom, and the Lord spoke of the tribulation in relation only to His earthly people; whereas from the standpoint of Patmos, He took account of the new element of Christendom.

But the words He spoke on Olivet were the words of God, and no dispensational change affects their eternal truth. And from them we learn that, when the time of their fulfillment comes, the Covenant people will have regained their normal status as the people of God, and that a believing community of Israelites will be living in their own land and their own "city," with a restored sanctuary accredited as "the Temple of God." Not "Jewish Christians" in the present-day sense, [2] but Jews whose faith will be akin to that of the Lord's disciples during His earthly ministry. And the very words which these disciples heard from the Master's lips will reach His disciples in that future age, just as they reach us today, by means of the printed page on which they are recorded.

> 2] For the Lord's coming for His heavenly people having already taken place, "the Christian Church" will have reached the full development of its apostasy, and will then be awaiting its fearful doom.

Once we shake free from the influence of traditional exegesis, we can see with noontide clearness that the entire scene, and all the circumstances, portrayed by the Lord's teaching in the 24th chapter of Matthew, pertain to the future age of a restored Israel. And therefore, prior to their fulfillment this "Christian dispensation" must have been brought to an end. And as it was in the past, so possibly it will be in the future, the change will be unheralded by any portents upon earth. But it will be ushered in by an event of vastly greater solemnity than any sights or sounds in the natural sphere. For then shall come the fulfillment of the word, "the Master of the house is risen up and hath shut to the door." The Lord will have passed from the throne of grace to the throne of judgment; and "the acceptable year of the Lord" will have run its course, and will soon be followed by "the day of vengeance of our God."

Great reserve is needed in attempting to map out the future as revealed in prophecy. But the Book of Daniel (9:27) tells us explicitly that the event predicted in Matthew 24:15 will take place in the middle of the 70th "week" of the prophetic era. And the Lord's words are perfectly explicit that the Tribulation will be followed immediately by the awful signs and portents which are to herald the coming of "the great and terrible day of the Lord" (Joel 2:31). But the 30th verse is commonly misread as though "the Coming of the Son of Man" were contemporaneous with the appearing of "the Sign of the Son of Man in heaven." So far from this being the case, the Lord's words which follow teach unmistakably that the "Coming", will be separated from the "Sign" by an interval sufficiently prolonged to allow the worldling to forget the awful portents of the coming judgments, and to make His people need exhortations to continued watchfulness. When verse 15 is fulfilled, His people will know that a definite period of three years and a half (1260 days) will bring the fulfillment of verse 29; but none save the Father Himself can tell when the Son of Man will come. Hence the significance of the warning, "The day of the Lord shall so come as a thief in the night." For it is "the coming of the Son of Man" that will usher in that awful period of judgment. [3] But let us not forget that Matthew 24:25 relate to the Coming of the Son of Man. In our hymnology, and indeed in our Christian literature generally, the Lord's names and titles are used just as the caprice of the writer, or the exigencies of rhythm or rhyme may suggest; but it is far otherwise in Scripture. And never once does the Lord's title of Son of Man occur in the Epistles of the New Testament: never once is it used in Scripture in relation to the Church of God or the people of God of this dispensation. Surely this fact alone might save us from the error of confounding the Coming of the Son of Man for the deliverance of His earthly people and the judgment of living nations upon earth, with the Coming of the Lord to call His heavenly people home, and to bring this "Christian dispensation" to an end.

> 3] As regards the 70 weeks, see NOTE at the end of chapter 3.

And yet the question will be asked in unison by many otherwise discordant voices, "Will not the Church pass through the tribulation?" If the question refers to the professing Church on earth, it has been already answered. [4] But if to the Church, the Body of Christ, it is unintelligent; for it ignores the great truths of the Christian revelation, noticed in preceding chapters. The Body of Christ is not on earth, nor can it have a corporate existence until the Divine purpose respecting it has been fulfilled. And moreover, as we have seen, the Lord's own teaching is most explicit, that a restored Israel will be, so to speak, the prime objective in that awful persecution; and a restored Israel implies the close of this Christian dispensation of grace.

> 4] At the Coming of the Lord, His own people within the professing Church will be called up to heaven, and that Church will be left to its doom. It may be asked again, "Will there be no longer any salvation for sinners within the apostate professing Church?" Surely the Divine principles of Romans 2:7 will hold good in that future age, as fully as in the past; and therefore, until "the great day of wrath" (which comes after the Tribulation) there will be mercy for those who seek it aright. Very many waverers, perhaps, will be startled into repentance by the Coming of the Lord.

Most strange it is that any Christian who studies the 24th chapter of Matthew can tolerate the thought that the Lord would tell us to live looking for His Coming, if intervening events barred the fulfillment of His words. For here in His teaching about His Coming as Son of Man, He warns His earthly people to look, not for His Coming, but for "things that must come to pass" before His Coming. And His words, "Watch, for ye know not what hour your Lord doth come," relate to a time when every intervening event has actually come to pass, and not a line of prophecy has to be fulfilled before His return.

And in view of all this we may surely ask, Would the Lord be less gracious - less true, I might almost add - in dealing with His heavenly people in this dispensation? We are taught to look for Him, and that a crowning blessing will be theirs "who are alive and remain unto the Coming of the Lord." Are we then to believe that this involves our passing through such times and scenes of terror as would make us "praise the dead that are already dead more than the living that are yet alive!" In his Patmos vision of that awful time the Seer hears a voice from heaven proclaiming, "Blessed are the dead." (Revelation 14:13) And if this Tribulation theory were true, should we not, in the spirit of those words, cry to God with earnest importunity to be allowed to die, rather than to await the Coming of the Lord?

And now we raise again the question, Are we who cling to the belief that the words of Holy Scripture mean what they seem to mean - are we the dupes of a blind delusion? Well, be it so. Some of us at least will cling to the delusion; and even if the "blessed hope" be no more than a happy dream, we shall refuse to change it for the hideous nightmare of "the Tribulation." But is it a delusion? The opening sentence of the present chapter may seem a startling statement. How was it then, some may ask, that all the early saints were led to expect the Lord's return? The answer is not far to seek. Never a week went by, never a Lord's day passed, without their hearing those charter words, "Until He come." And who among them could fail to ask their meaning! Whatever else of Christian truth they lacked, this at least they knew from the day they first took part in the sacred rite - the Lord who died for them would return again, and they were to live looking for His Coming.

CHAPTER 9

MEANTIME, THE CHURCH AGE

"MY people doth not consider." Such was the reproach cast upon Israel in the days of Isaiah's prophecy. And surely a like reproach rests upon the people of God today in regard to the promise of the Lord's return. During all His ministry He spoke of His coming again; and He confirmed the promise after His resurrection from the dead. The teaching of His inspired Apostles gave prominence to the hope. And in His final message to His people, as recorded on the last page of Scripture, the words are three times repeated, "I am coming quickly."

"Surely I am coming quickly." No reference here to a thousand-year day of the eternal God, but to the time calendars of men. "The time was long," was Daniel's lament as he pondered the revelation made to him, that seven times seventy years would pass before the realization of the promised blessings to his people. And more than four centuries elapsed between the promise of the land to Abraham, and the day when his descendants took possession of it. But nineteen centuries! And in view of such a promise, "Surely I am coming quickly"! Here it would be the pettiest quibble to raise the question of the Tribulation - persecution definitely limited to a term that might be covered twenty times within a single lifetime. At this point, then, let us turn aside from controversy. Let us awake to realities and think. And if we do but think, the staggering fact of a nineteen centuries' delay will lead us to "consider" with a solemnity and earnestness we have never known before.

Under the guidance of the Holy Spirit, given to "lead them into all truth," the Apostles taught the saints to look for the Coming as a present hope. The suggestion of subterfuge or mistake would be profane. The facts are not in dispute. how then can they be explained? Israel's story may teach us something here. When the people were encamped at Sinai, Canaan lay but a few days' march across the desert. And in the second year from the Exodus, they were led to the borders of the land, and bidden to enter and take possession of it. "But they entered not in because of unbelief." The Canaan rest, moreover, was only a type of the promised rest of the Messianic Kingdom. That rest was preached again "in David," (Hebrews 4:7) but lost again through unbelief and the apostasy which unbelief begets. And in the exile it was revealed to Daniel that it would be further deferred for seven times seventy years. Lastly it was preached at Pentecost, and lost once more by unbelief. And to continued unbelief is due the fact of these nineteen centuries of Israel's rejection. Does not this throw light on the seeming failure of "the hope of the Church"? Putting from us the profane thought that the Lord has been unmindful of His promise, are we not led to the conclusion that this long delay has been due to the unfaithfulness of His people upon earth? The third chapter of 2 Peter has no bearing upon the question. In that passage the Apostle is not dealing with either the hopes or the heresies of Christians, but with the scoffing of the unbeliever who mocks at the Divine warning that the world shall at last be given up to judgment fire. The scientist may possibly be right in thinking that "for untold millions of years this earth has been the theatre of life and death." [1] All that we know is that "in the beginning" (whenever that was) God created it, and that He did not create it "a waste," albeit it had become a waste (Isaiah 45:18, R.V. Cf. Genesis 1:2, R. V.,) [2] before the epoch of the Adamic creation. And 2 Peter 3:5, 6, points to the cataclysm referred to in Genesis 1:2, by which "the world that then was, being overflowed with water, perished."

1] The words are Professor Tyndall's.

2] The same Hebrew word is used.

"Where is the promise of His coming!" is not the appeal of an inquirer as to the Coming of Christ, but the taunt of a scoffer about the coming of "the day of God." [3] And the Apostle answers his appeal to the permanence of "all things from the beginning of the creation" by referring to the aeons of Genesis 1:2, and to a God with whom a thousand years are as one day. [4] But what bearing can this passage in Peter's Epistle have upon the question here at issue? The long-suffering of God explains His tiding back the sea of fire by which the world is at last to be engulfed, but it cannot explain the Lord's delaying to fulfill His promise to His believing people. "The coming of the day of God" means endless destruction for all the ungodly inhabitants of the earth; whereas beyond the coming of the Lord Jesus there lies the fulfillment of the hope of Israel, which is to be "as life from the dead" to the nations of the earth; and beyond that again there lies the deliverance of a groaning creation.

> 3] It is an exclamation, like Galatians 4:15. And announcement is the primary and common meaning of the word here translated "promise." It might be freely rendered, "What has become of His announcement?"

> 4] The conflict between science and Scripture in regard to Genesis 1 is mainly due to misreading Genesis. It does not describe the creation of the earth, but its refurnishing as a home for man.

No, no; the question here cannot be solved in that way. Nor can we tolerate the thought that the promise has failed. Sometimes in the past, God has not fulfilled His word, but only when His word threatened wrath. (See, e.g., Exodus 32:11-14; Joshua 3:10) No Divine promise of blessing has ever failed. But if we reject that solution of the difficulty, what other can be found? No event or influence of a transient nature deserves a moment's consideration; nothing partial or merely local in its effects. We must find a cause of which the influence began to be felt before the Apostles left the earth, and which has been in operation during all the centuries until the present hour. And by a process of negative induction the suggestion forces itself upon us that the evil history of the Church on earth may afford a solution of the mystery.

Christian thought, I again repeat it, is leavened with the error of failing to distinguish between the heavenly Church and the Church on earth. But here I would fain shirk the role of an iconoclast, and I will shelter myself behind the. words of others in seeking to expose the prevalent; superstitions to which that error has given rise,, superstitions which are inconsistent with undivided loyalty to our Lord Jesus Christ. The following sentences are quoted from Canon T. D. Bernard's Bampton Lectures of 1864, [5] a great book which ought to find a place in every Christian library:

> 5] The Progress of Doctrine in the New Testament (Macmillan & Co.). I had the satisfaction of appealing successfully for the reissue of this book a dozen years ago.

"How fair was the morning of the Church! how swift its progress! what expectations it would have been natural to form of the future history which had begun so well! Doubtless they were formed in many a sanguine heart but they were clouded soon... "While the Apostles wrote, the actual state and the visible tendencies of things showed too plainly what Church history would be; and at the same time prophetic intimations made the prospect still more dark...

"I know not how any man in closing the Epistles could expect to find the subsequent history of the Church essentially different from what it is. In those writings we seem, as it were, not to witness some passing storms which clear the air, but to feel the whole atmosphere charged with the elements of future tempest and death...

"The fact which I observe is not merely that these indications of the future are in the Epistles, but that they increase as we approach the close; and after the doctrines of the Gospel have been fully wrought out, and the fullness of personal salvation and the ideal character of the Church have been placed in the clearest light, the shadows gather and deepen on the external history. The last words of St. Paul in the second Epistle to Timothy, and those of St. Peter in his second Epistle, with the Epistles of St. John and St. Jude, breathe the language of a time in which the tendencies of that history had distinctly shown themselves; and in this respect these writings form a prelude and a passage to the Apocalypse."

The Church's story from the close of the New Testament Canon to the era of the Patristic theologians must be gleaned from the revelations their writings afford of its condition in their own time. Who can doubt that then, as in the days of Israel's apostasy, there were many who feared the Lord and thought upon His name? But here I am speaking of the Church as a whole. Protestantism delights in attributing to the Romish apostasy the vices which disgraced the Church of Christendom during the Middle Ages; but in this regard the Church of Rome was merely the product and development of the much-vaunted "primitive Church" of the Fathers. Abundant proof of this will be found in the acts and words of some of the great and holy men who sought in vain to stem the evil tide. The facts are disclosed in various standard works; here of course s few characteristic extracts must suffice.

The birth of Cyprian occurred about a century after the death of the last of the Apostles. Born and bred in Paganism, he was converted in middle age, and three years afterwards he became Bishop of Carthage. Ten years later he suffered martyrdom in the Valerian persecution. The following words may indicate the condition of the Church in his time -"Serious scandals existed even among the clergy. Bishops were farmers, traders, and moneylenders, and by no means always honest. Some were too ignorant to teach the catechumens. Presbyters made money by helping in the manufacture of idols." [6]

> 6] Dr. Plummer's Church of the Early Fathers, chapter 7.

In Cyprian's day "the virgins of the Church" ("nuns" we call them now) were held in special honor on account of their reputed sanctity. What, then, passed for superior sanctity may be gleaned from the following words of that eminent and holy man - "What have the virgins of the Church to do at promiscuous baths, there to violate the commonest dictates of feminine modesty! The places you frequent are more filthy than the theatre itself; all modesty is there laid aside; and with your robes your personal honor and reserve are cast off." [7] Half a century before these words were written, Clement of Alexandria had bewailed the low morality which prevailed among Christians, even at a time when, as he said, "the wells of martyrdom were flowing daily." Referring to their attendance at church he wrote: "After having waited upon God and heard of Him, they leave Him there, and find their pleasure without in ungodly fiddling, and love songs, and what-not - stage plays and gross revelries."

7 De Habitu Virgimum.

The "conversion of Constantine" set free the Church to put her house in order, and pursue her mission to the world without hindrance from without. But her condition in those halcyon days may be judged by the fact that at a single visitation the great Chrysostom deposed no fewer than thirteen bishops for simony and licentiousness. Nor was this strange, having regard to the means by which men secured election to the episcopal office. Here are Chrysostom's words: "That some have filled the churches with murders, and made cities desolate when contending for this position, I now pass over, lest I should seem to say what is incredible to any." He was equally unsparing in dealing with the vices of the lower orders of the clergy. The natural result followed. The "historic Church" convened a packed council, which deprived him of his archbishopric, and he was banished to Nicaea. Moved, however, by the indignant fury of the laity, the Emperor recalled him, and his return to Constantinople was like a public triumph. But his fearless and scathing denunciations of the corruptions and immoralities of Church and Court led to the summoning of another council, more skillfully arranged; and his second banishment was intended to be, as in fact it proved, a death sentence. He practically died a martyr - one of the first of the great army whose blood cries to God for vengeance upon the "historic Church."

Nor were licentiousness and simony evils of recent growth in the Church; nor were they peculiar to the see of Chrysostom. In A. D. 870 an imperial edict was read in the churches of Rome, prohibiting clerics and monks from resorting to the houses of widows or female wards, and making them "incapable of receiving anything from the liberality or will of any woman to whom they may attach themselves under the plea of religion; and (the edict adds) any such donations or legacies as they shall have appropriated to themselves shall be confiscated."

This edict, sweeping though its terms were, had to be confirmed and strengthened by another twenty years later. And here is the comment of Jerome on the subject: "I blush to say it, heathen priests, players of pantomimes, drivers of chariots in the circuses, and harlots are allowed to receive legacies; clergy and monks are forbidden to do so by Christian princes. Nor do I complain of the law (he adds), but I am grieved that we deserve it." [8] According to Jerome, so great was the evil, that men actually sought ordination in order to gain easier access to the society of women, and to trade upon their credulity. He, at least, maintained no reserve about the vices of the clergy of his day. And the picture he draws of the state of female society among the Christians is so repulsive that, as a recent writer remarks, we would gladly believe it to be exaggerated; but (he adds) "if the priesthood, with its enormous influence, was so corrupt, it is only too probable that it debased the sex which is always most under clerical influence." [9]

8 Wordsworth's Church History, vol. 3. p. 92.

9] Dill's Roman, Society, p. 113.

Of "Saint" Cyril of Alexandria, Dean Milman writes' "While ambition, intrigue, arrogance, rapacity, and violence are proscribed as unchristian means, barbarity, persecution, bloodshed, as unholy and unevangelical wickednesses, posterity will condemn this orthodox Cyril as one of the worst of heretics against the spirit of the Gospel."

A kindly estimate this, of a man who was morally guilty of the murder of Hypatia, and who was a notorious mob leader, and the brutal persecutor of the Jews, whom he drove out of Alexandria in thousands, giving up their houses to pillage. This turbulent pagan claims notice here only because he was the ruling spirit in the Council of Ephesus (A.D. 481), which dealt with the heresies of Nestorius. Cyril had hurled anathemas against him for refusing to acknowledge the Virgin Mary as the "Mother of God," and he procured his condemnation by means that would discredit the lowest political contest, including the free use of a hired mob. So disgraceful was the disorder which prevailed that the Emperor dissolved the Council with the rebuke' "God is my witness that I am not the author of this confusion. His providence will discover and punish the guilty. Return to your provinces, and may your private virtues repair the mischief and scandal of your meeting." [10]

> 10] And this was one of the "Ecumenical Councils" which were recognized in England even after the Reformation. At the Ephesus Council of eighteen years later the "orthodox" majority made free use of their hired bullies, and Flavian, Bishop of Byzantium, received such brutal treatment that he died of his injuries. As another illustration of what, in his Bampton Lectures, Canon Liddon calls "the illuminated mind of primitive Christendom," it may be mentioned that in the struggle for the Popedom between the rival factions of Damasus and Ursinus, 131 corpses were left on the pavement of one of the Roman churches in a single day.

No one need suppose that a wider outlook would lead us to reverse the judgment to which these facts and testimonies point. A portly volume would not contain the evidence available to prove the utter apostasy of "the primitive Church of the Fathers." One more testimony, however, is all I will here adduce. In his early life Salvian of Marseilles was the contemporary of Jerome and Augustine, the greatest of all the Latin Fathers. A century had elapsed since "the conversion of Constantine." The "persecution" which the Christians had most to fear from the State was due to their vices and crimes, and to the operation of penal laws of drastic severity, designed to prevent their lapsing back to paganism. Why was it then that God seemed to have forsaken the Church? Here is Salvian's answer – "See what Christians actually are everywhere, and then ask whether, under the administration of a righteous and holy God, such men can expect any favor? What happens every day under our very eyes is rather an evidence of the doctrine of Providence, as it displays the Divine displeasure provoked by the debauchery of the Church itself." The following are further extracts from the same treatise:

> "How can we wonder that God does not hearken to our prayers…Alas! how grievous and doleful is what I have to say!

The very Church of God, which ought to be the appeaser of God, is but the provoker of God. And a very few excepted who flee from evil, what is almost every assembly of Christians but a sink of vices. For you will find in the Church scarcely one who is not either a drunkard or a glutton, or an adulterer, or a fornicator or frequenter of brothels, or a robber or a murderer. I put it now to the consciences of all Christian people whether it be not so...

"The Churches are outraged by indecencies...You may well imagine what men have been thinking about at church when you see them hurry off, some to plunder, some to get drunk, some to practice lewdness, some to rob on the highway...

"How should we exult and leap for joy if we could believe that the good and bad were nearly balanced in the Church as to numbers!...How happy should we be in so thinking, but in fact we have to mourn over almost the whole mass as guilty."

In accounting for the growth of Christianity in early days, Gibbon the infidel gives prominence to the morality of the Christians. And Tertullian declared that no one who transgressed the rules of Christian discipline and propriety was recognized as a Christian at all. And yet two centuries later, "almost every assembly of Christians had become a sink of vices!" [11]

11] The body of Salvian's treatise containing this terrible indictment of the Primitive Church is given in Taylor's Ancient Christianity, together with quotations from Augustine and others of the Fathers in support of his testimony. The preceding clauses are taken from The Buddha of Christendom now republished as The Bible or the Church.

There is no need in this connection to speak of the Church of the Middle Ages - the fiendish enemy and persecutor of all who feared the Lord and followed righteousness and truth. The estimates formed of the number of the martyrs are unreliable; for though not one of those many millions is forgotten in heaven, the records on earth are altogether faulty. This at least is certain, that for long ages God was on the side of the martyrs, and that the Church of Christendom was the most awful impersonation of the powers of hell that earth has ever known. "No means came amiss to it, sword or stake, torture chamber or assassin's dagger. The effects of the Church's working were seen in ruined nations and smoking cities, in human beings tearing one another to pieces, like raging maniacs, and the honor of the Creator of the world befouled by the hideous crimes committed in His name. All this is forgotten now, forgotten and even audaciously denied." [12]

12] Froude's Council of Trent.

And what of the Churches of the Reformation? Here I will call another witness whose words should command attention. The following is a quotation from Dean Alford's Commentary on the Lord's Parable recorded in Matthew 12:48-44. After explaining the direct application of the parable to the Jewish people, he proceeds:

"Strikingly parallel with this runs the history of the Christian Church. Not long after the apostolic times, the golden calves of idolatry were set up by the Church of Rome. What the effect of the captivity was to the Jews, that of the Reformation has been to Christendom. The first evil spirit has been cast out. But by the growth of hypocrisy, secularity, and rationalism, the house has become empty, swept, and garnished by the decencies of civilization and discoveries of secular knowledge, but empty of living and earnest faith. And he must read prophecy but ill, who does not see under all these seeming improvements the preparation for the final development of the man of sin, the great repossession when idolatry and the seven worse spirits shall bring the outward frame of so-called Christendom to a fearful end."

With what increased emphasis might Dean Alford write these words today if he were still with us! Half a century ago the Church of England was giving a bold testimony to the principles of the Reformation, or, in other words, to the Divine authority of Scripture, and the great truths which Scripture teaches. And Nonconformity was a great spiritual power throughout the land. But today the Epistle to Laodicea is finding its fulfillment on every hand. For though "empty of living and earnest faith," the Churches were never so boastful of their condition. "The tree of knowledge, now, yields its last, ripest fruit," for men sit in judgment on the Word of God!

The Philadelphian Epistle promised an open door that none could shut; and at the Reformation the Bible was given to the people. The Devil has thus been baffled for centuries; for a return to his former methods is barred by the printing-press. But quite as effectually, and by far more subtle means, the Old Serpent is now filching the Bible from us. It is acclaimed as the best of books, but it is not the Word of God. And the agency by which he is seeking to achieve this fell design is the same as that which he used in pre-Reformation times - the Professing Church on earth.

And the Churches of the Reformation are his chief agents in this evil work. Within living memory they stood together in defence of the Bible, but there is not one of them that corporately maintains that testimony today. Stier's epigram about the teaching of German Rationalists applies to the teaching of most of our Theological Colleges and numberless quasi-Christian pulpits - "Heaven and earth will never pass away, but the words of Christ pass away in time!"

Some one may object, perhaps, that all this refers only to the Professing Church, and not to the true Church. But there are not two Churches on earth in this dispensation, any more than in that which preceded it. "The Jewish Church" was Divine in its origin, but it was apostate; and so is it with the Church on earth today. The only true Church is that which the Lord is building, and it has no corporate existence upon earth. But it may be said that the real Christians, though within the Professing Church, are in no way responsible for its apostasy. In the age of the martyrs this plea might, perhaps, have been sustained, but never before or since. And certainly not today; for their apathy amounts in effect to positive connivance with evils which are undermining true Christianity. If they stood together in refusing to enter any church in which an altar, with its pagan furniture, has supplanted the Communion Table, or where, in the ministry of the pulpit, the "Higher Criticism" has dethroned the Word of

God, the very apostasy itself might prove a blessing in disguise. But faithfulness to the Lord is subordinated to the maintenance of "Church unity." And so "the salt has lost its savour," and all hope of recovery is gone.

It seems to be forgotten that discipleship is a personal bond. "Follow Me" is not addressed to congregations, but to the individual Christian. To love father or mother more than Christ is to be unworthy of Him; but it is deemed allowable to love one's Church more than Him? In the Epistles to the Seven Churches, from Ephesus to Laodicea, the ruling note is individual faithfulness - "to him that overcometh." A similar note vibrates in the Apostle Paul's address to the Elders of Ephesus. The future of the Church was dark. Grievous wolves would enter in among them, and of their own selves there would arise fomenters of heresy and leaders of schism. And what was to be their resource? "I commend you to God and to the word of His grace." (Acts 20:29-32)

It marks a crisis in the Apostle's ministry. His earlier Epistles had been addressed to churches; but Ephesians, Colossians, Philippians, written during his Roman imprisonment, were addressed to "saints." In sympathy with the Apostle's words, Chrysostom, writing three centuries later, lamented that "all things which are Christ's in the truth" were counterfeited in the prevailing heresies of that age, and he urged that Christians "should betake themselves only to the Scriptures." And in our own day all this found an echo in the exhortation of the late Bishop Ryle, that Christians should expect nothing from churches, but look only to the Lord.

The student of human nature who has adequate means and opportunities of inquiry respecting the vices and crimes of men finds no need of a devil to account for everything in that sphere. But, without the Satan of Scripture, the religion of men is an insoluble enigma. For Satan is the god of this world, and therefore the religion of the world is the normal sphere of his activities. And, as Luther said, all his assaults are aimed at Christ Himself. He blinds the minds of men to the revelation of a Christ who is "the image of God." (2 Corinthians 4:4-6) The Deity of Christ is thus his main objective, for upon that depends everything that is vital in Christianity.

Hence his campaign against the Bible. For no one whose mind is not warped or blinded by the superstitions of religion can fail to recognize that it is only through the written Word that we can reach "the living Word." The man who denies the Divine authority and inspiration of Holy Scripture and yet clings to a belief in the atonement of Calvary and the Deity of Christ is a superstitious creature who would believe anything. [13]

> 13] Since these pages were written, a sadder book even than Newman's Apologia has been published, viz. Monsignor Benson's Confessions of a Convert. The fact that such men as these are led by the prevalent superstitions about "the Church" to make shipwreck of their Christian life proves the need of plain speaking on this subject. And surely all who are connected with either of the historic Churches of the Reformation have a peculiar right, if not a special responsibility, to undertake the unwelcome task.

CHAPTER 10
WHY THE DELAY?

FULL well I know that the preceding chapter will give offence and be resented. [1] But having regard to the awfully solemn import of the question here at issue, considerations of that kind must be ignored. For what concerns us is whether the lapse of nineteen centuries gives proof that the Lord has been false to His promise, or whether the history of the Professing Church during all the centuries, down to the present hour, does not amply explain why the fulfillment of His promise is delayed. Coupled with the promise are the words in which He expects His people to respond - "Even so, come, Lord Jesus." But there is not one of the Churches of the Reformation that would corporately identify itself with that prayer. And the Church that claims to be the Divine oracle and interpreter of Scripture, displays its enlightenment by an error that might disgrace a schoolboy, for it interprets the Lord's words about "the consummation of the age" to mean the end of the world. The blunder is as crassly ignorant as that of finding in the parable of the tares a warrant for murdering the martyrs. But the Churches of the Reformation, while of course rejecting the heresy which found expression in the fires of Smithfield, have adopted the heresy which relegates the "Second Advent" to the "end of the world"; and as the result (to quote Bengel's words) "the Churches have forgotten the hope of the Church."

> 1] In these days to hold that the Lord of glory was duped by Jewish superstitions about the Divine authority of Holy Scripture is proof of enlightenment, but a man is "past praying for" who exposes the pestilent superstitions about the Church, which are the stock-in-trade of the Apostasy!

And yet the Coming is inseparably linked with the Cross. Much there is in Scripture that the thoughtless can ignore; but not the words, "Ye do shew the Lord's death till He come." The many who dismiss the Coming to the end of all things, would presumably wish us to believe that, at the Lord's Supper, the cup which points back to the blood of our redemption, points forward to the blood of Isaiah's prophecy of "the day of vengeance"; and some who are too enlightened for this would find us a half-way house amid the horrors of the Great Tribulation. But all this betokens either ignorance of Scripture, or a mistaken exegesis. "Till He come" the words are an implicit renewal of the promise, and an appeal to every heart that has learned by grace to look for "that blessed hope." Doctrines are for the head, but the heart reaches out to a person; and here it is Himself that the Lord brings before His people. "This do in remembrance of ME." - not the Christ of the crucifix, not a dead Christ, but an absent Lord who has promised to come again.

But here the ways divide, and we must choose between the teachings of theologians of repute and the words of Holy Scripture. In the 11th chapter of I Corinthians, the Apostle declares that the Church's charter relative to the Lord's Supper had been specially revealed to him, and he proceeds to deliver to them what he had thus "received of the Lord." And yet here is what a great commentator has to say upon the 26th verse "The words are addressed directly to the Corinthians, not to them and all succeeding Christians; the Apostle regarding the coming of the Lord as near at hand, in his own time." [2]

2] Dean Alford in loco. The italics are his own.

Many a page might be filled with quotations from other eminent divines, all testifying to the fact that the Lord's return was a present hope with the early saints, and offering a similar explanation of the seeming falseness of that hope. The momentous question here under consideration is thus disposed of by the assumption that, in regard to this vital truth, the Apostles were in error, and misled the Church entrusted to their care. I repeat, therefore, that here we reach a parting of the ways; for we cannot consent to escape from a difficulty by undermining faith in Holy Scripture. "Gird up the loins of your mind" is a much-needed exhortation, and in no sphere more than in relation to this very truth. For let us face the facts once again. The inspired Apostles taught their converts to expect the Lord's return. And "I am coming quickly" was His own last message to His people, before the era of revelation ended, and the era of a silent heaven set in. But He did not come quickly, nor has He come at all. Were it not for the "slovenly-mindedness" that characterizes thought in the religious sphere, this overwhelming fact would lead to searchings of heart on the part of all spiritual Christians.

Scattered among the various Churches there must surely be very many who cherish the hope, and are troubled at the Lord's continued absence. And is it idle to suggest that they should come together for earnest inquiry and prayer upon this subject? Even in the dark days of Elijah's prophecy, there were 7000 true-hearted seekers after God in Israel; is it possible then that, in this seven-million peopled London, there are not seven thousand Christians who would eagerly devote a day to such a purpose! And let them be of one mind. Opinions may differ as to which phase of His Coming the Lord had in view in His parting message, and as to whether any events must precede the fulfillment of it. But in presence of the fact that we are in the twentieth century of the Christian era, to raise questions of this kind would betoken a spirit of controversy or of mere quibbling. In regard to what Bengel calls "the hope of the Church" let us have an *eirenicon*. It is sad that truth which ought to unite all spiritual Christians should lead to strife. And the fault is not all on one side. "The secret rapture," "the Coming of the Lord for His Church," "His coming back with His Church" - these and other kindred phrases are used as though they expressed revealed truth, whereas they express mere inferences from Scripture, which may be true or may be false.

The Fourth Gospel closes with an incident which every Bible student ought to study. On receiving the command, "Follow Me," Peter pointed to his companion and asked, "What shall this man do?" And his inquiry brought the Lord's rebuke, "If I will that he tarry till I come, what is that to thee?" How natural the inference the disciples drew, "that that disciple should not die"! What other inference would anyone draw? But the Evangelist cites the Lord's words a second time, in order to make it clear that He did not say what the disciples inferred to be His meaning. And the moral is that in all such matters we are not to draw inferences from Divine words, but to accept them with childlike simplicity.

The language of Zechariah 14:4 and Acts 1:11 may seem to indicate that the Coming there foretold will be secret, in the sense in which the Ascension was secret - with no attendant angels, no manifestation to the world. But of another Coming it is said, "Every eye shall see Him." And if some sceptic demands how that is possible on this round earth, let him ask the first schoolboy he meets how it is that, day by day, every eye can see the sun! When "the King of Glory passes on his way," then, "From earth's wide bounds, from ocean's furthest coast," "every eye shall see Him." But whether this will be true of the Coming of "that blessed hope" Scripture does not tell us; and we must not corrupt or add to Scripture with our own inferences and "pious opinions."

Scripture teaches explicitly that, after this Christian dispensation ends, Israel will be restored to Divine favour; and the question is sometimes asked, how this will be brought about - "How can they hear without a preacher?" for, ex-hypothesi, all Christians will previously have been called away to heaven. And in our day-dreams the thought arises at times whether the devout among His earthly people may not see Him when He comes to call His heavenly people home. But this is a day-dream, nothing more.

Then as regards the Lord's coming for His Church, the phrase is incorrect, not merely on grounds already indicated, but also because it seems to imply that none of the holy dead of former ages will have part in that resurrection; and for this we have no Scriptural warrant. Not that we would dare to assert the contrary. It behooves us to know whatever the Scripture teaches, and to be content not to know where Scripture is silent. And this applies no less to the theory of His coming back with His Church. Here again some of us have day-dreams. May it not be that "the holy ones" of His glorious escort, when He comes to execute vengeance upon earth, will be "the angels of His power," and that the redeemed of this age of grace will have no part in that dread ministry?

Allied with this is that other phrase, "the personal reign of Christ on earth"; as though the Lord of glory is ever to live in a palace in Jerusalem! In our day-dreams here, the redeemed of the heavenly glory are not upon the earth, but with the Lord as He reigns over the earth. Not in a heaven "beyond the stars," but in a heaven as near as it seemed to be in the Patmos visions, or when the martyr Stephen's eyes were opened to behold it. But these again are only dreams; and men who dogmatize on these subjects are quite as silly, though neither as harmless nor as interesting, as a set of babies in the nursery, prattling about things that are beyond their ken.

These criticisms and suggestions are designed merely to eliminate certain elements that tend either to prejudice, or to obscure, the consideration of the question here at issue. We often wonder that the Jews are not startled into repentance by the fact that, though we have reached the twentieth century of the Christian era, their national hope is still unfulfilled. And are we to remain indifferent to the fact that our Christian hope is also unrealized? "Yet a very little while and the Coming One will come and will not tarry": (Hebrews 10:37) such words as these cannot be explained away by the theory of a thousand-years' day. What then should be our action and our attitude in this matter?

Has the past no lesson for us? "The Jewish Church" had a right creed, and the coming of Messiah was a vital part of it. But with the "Church" as a Church it was merely a doctrine. They did not want Him; and when He came they cast Him out. It was only with the few that it was a hope, and a heart-longing hope. They were really looking for Him - "waiting for the consolation of Israel," like the old saint who took the infant Saviour in his arms and said, "Now, Lord, lettest Thou Thy servant depart in peace...for mine eyes have seen Thy salvation." They had a divinely appointed "Church," with a ritual divinely ordered in every detail. And the Lord took His place within it, as did the disciples under His teaching. But though in it, they were not of it. "The existing communities, the religious tendencies, the spirit of the age, assuredly offered no point of attachment, only absolute and essential contrariety, to the kingdom of heaven." [3]

3] These words are Dr. Alfred Edersheim's.

And this has its parallel today. Ministers and congregations that cling to "the faith once delivered," reverencing the Scriptures as the Word of God, and cherishing the hope which the Scriptures inspire, find themselves daily more and more out of sympathy with the "organized Christianity" of which they are outwardly a part. In these "latter times," strikingly characterized, as they are, by "departing from the faith," the unity of the Church can be promoted only by giving up the faith, and truckling to rationalism and ritualism. But "to keep the unity of the Spirit" ought to be the aspiration and the aim of all who are true to Christ. And this is the true "Communion of Saints" - "not the common performance of external acts, but a communion of soul with soul, and of the soul with Christ. It is a consequence of the nature which God has given us that an external organization should help our communion with one another. But subtler, deeper, diviner, than anything of which external things can be either the symbol or the bond is that inner reality and essence of union - 'the unity of the Spirit.'" [4]

4] Hatch's Bampton Lectures, 1880 (vii.).

And no influence can be more fitted to promote this unity than the confession of a common hope, and the longing which the hope inspires. No need here, moreover, for large assemblies or eloquent exhortations. Enthusiasm thus produced is transient. And He Himself it was who spoke of the "two or three" gathered together in His name. Among Christians everywhere there must surely be some "who love His appearing." And if today, for the first time in all the sad history of Christendom, such would come together in every place the wide world over, wherever Christians can be found, we might look up in hope that He who is called "The Coming One" [5] would fulfill the promise of His name.

5] (Greek). — Hebrews 10:37.

CHAPTER 11

"BEMA" OF CHRIST

IN the Apostle Paul's farewell words to Timothy there is nothing more pathetic than his reference to the hope. In the school of grace he had learned to live looking for the Lord's appearing. (Titus 2:11-13) But now he writes, "the time of my departure is at hand." Perhaps it had been revealed to him, as it was revealed to Peter, that he was about to be "offered up" - to die a martyr's death. But this gives rise to no suspicions of his having been misled respecting the hope, or of his having misled the converts. The only change in his language is the use of a new verb and a different tense. He had been looking for the appearing; now, he speaks of having loved it. And taking his place with all who, like himself, would have to enter the promised land through the waters of the Jordan, he says "Henceforth there is laid up for me the crown of righteousness, which the Lord, the righteous judge, shall give me at that day and not only to me, but also to all them that have loved His appearing." (2 Timothy 4:8) In connection with his epigram already quoted, Bengel notices that, in the New Testament, exhortations to faithfulness are based upon the hope of the Coming. And the failure of Christian life is largely due to the fact that the truth of grace is commonly separated from that hope. A certain great Jewish Rabbi astonished his disciples by teaching that every man should repent the day before his death. How, they asked him, could they know the day of their death? They could not know it, was his reply, and therefore every one should act as if each day was his last. If men could count on a few years' warning of death, "deathbed repentances" would become the rule. And certain it is that if great events foretold in Hebrew prophecy must precede the Lord's return, His coming will have less power to mould the character and influence the life than it had in Apostolic times. In these strange days of "stress and strain," cases of" loss of memory" are becoming frequent. People are "found wandering." Who they are, and where they came from, they cannot tell. Their past is all a blank; they remember nothing. And many Christians expect to reach heaven in that condition. The cloud on which they will be poised, as they sing the New Song of the redeemed, will shut out every memory of life on earth, with its unnumbered mercies and its unnumbered sins! Some there are, again, whose case is like that of another famous Rabbi, who, when he came to die, burst into tears through fear of Divine judgment; and when his disciples who stood around his deathbed expressed surprise that he, "the light of Israel," should be a prey to such misgivings, he told them that he knew not by which of the two roads his journey lay, to Paradise or to Gehenna.

Most Christians seem to oscillate between these two extremes of error. Many are strangers to settled peace, because they fear to trust "the word of the truth of the Gospel." And those who know what it means to have "a heart established by grace" need to be reminded of the solemnities of the judgment-seat of Christ. For this subject of the judgment of the redeemed falls within the category of neglected truths.

Chrysostom's exposition of the 5th chapter of 2 Corinthians has been described as "one of the grandest efforts of human eloquence." But, intensely Christian though he was in heart and life, that great saint and teacher misread the Apostle's words. And the mistranslation of the passage in our English version is a testimony to the far-reaching influence of his brilliant homily. To be "accepted of Him" is not the aim of the Christian life, nor is "the terror of the Lord" its constraining motive. For "the judgment-seat of Christ" is not the dread tribunal of "the great white throne" of the Patmos vision. The "we" of the tenth verse is the of all the verses that precede and follow it. The whole passage breathes confidence and courage. God has "wrought" us for immortality, and He has given us the Holy Spirit as the earnest of that which is our assured destiny. And it is to us that the entire chapter refers. Here are the Apostle's words:

"Being therefore always of good courage, and knowing that, whilst we are at home in the body, we are absent from the Lord (for we walk by faith, not by sight); we are of good courage, I say, and are willing rather to be absent from the body, and to be at home with the Lord. Wherefore also we make it our aim, whether at home or absent, to be well-pleasing unto Him. For we must all be made manifest before the judgment-seat of Christ; that each one may receive the things done in the body, according to what he hath done, whether it be good or bad. Knowing therefore the fear of the Lord, we persuade men, but we are made manifest unto God; and I hope that we are made manifest also in your consciences." (2 Corinthians 5:6-11)

The salvation of the soul is not a prize to be won by saintship, but a blessing bestowed by Divine grace upon the sinner who believes in the Lord Jesus Christ. It is not the goal, but the starting-point, of the Christian's life. Upon two main points the teaching of Scripture is explicit; the consequences of accepting or rejecting Christ are eternal; and the destiny of all will be declared by the resurrection. For the resurrection will be either "unto life" or unto judgment; and the saved will be raised in bodies "fashioned like unto His glorious body." And it is as thus; "raised in glory" that we shall be judged.

This disposes of the Patristic interpretation of the passage, by which our translators were misled. Even the word "appear" lends itself to the error, for it suggests arraignment before it criminal tribunal on the issue of guilty or not guilty, whereas the "resurrection unto life" will be a public proof that every question of guilt has been for ever settled. The judgment of 2 Corinthians 5:10 will possibly be a public manifestation of the Father's judgment of 1 Peter 1:17, which is at present a secret matter between the child of God and his heavenly Father. Perhaps, indeed, the forensic tone given to the passage by the word "judgment-seat" may be foreign to its intention. [1]

> 1] The primary meaning of behma is a space on which to put one's foot, as in Acts 7:5; then, a raised place, a platform or pulpit, as in Nehemiah 8:4 (LXX). This is its usual meaning in classical Greek. Then, a throne (Acts 12:21) and a judgment-seat.

This suggestion is greatly strengthened by the Revised Text, where "bad" is displaced by phaulos - one of those words, as Archbishop Trench notices, "which contemplate evil under another aspect, that, namely, of its good-for-nothingness." And, he adds, "This notion of worthlessness is the central notion of phaulos," though the word runs through other meanings until it reaches "bad"; "but still bad predominantly in the sense of worthless." [2]

> 2] N.T. Synonyms, Second Series. In his concluding sentence he says, "The severer meaning is involved in the word in other places in the New Testament where it occurs." The primary meaning of the word, according to Grimm, is "easy, slight, ordinary, mean, worthless, of no account."

All this immensely deepens both the scope and the solemnity of the Apostle's words. Many who could say with him, "I know nothing against myself," miss the significance of what he adds - "yet am I not hereby justified, but He that judgeth me is the Lord." And the Apostle Peter's words about a "vain (or resultless) manner of life" come to mind in this connection. (1 Peter 1:18) Writing to Hebrew Christians, his words refer to the strictly moral and religious life that characterized devout Judaism after the Ezra revival. And are there not very many pious people nowadays who, though leading exemplary lives, will have no garnered sheaves "against that day"?

I deprecate the thought that I wish to fritter away the solemn truth of the bema of Christ. My purpose is merely to explain the words in which it has been revealed. For the passage has been so perverted that even the word "receive" is commonly read with a police-court flavour attaching to it. (The following are the passages where it occurs: Matthew 25:27; Luke 7:37 (brought); 2 Corinthians 5:10; Ephesians 6:8; Colossians 3:25; Hebrews 10:36; 11:19, 39; 1 Peter 1:9; 5:4; 2 Peter 2:13.) And this leads to efforts to get rid of the truth altogether. Such efforts are as discreditable as they are vain. Even in this life no one of generous feeling can fail to be distressed by the consciousness that he is unworthy of the estimate his fellows form of him; and he is always glad to be "made manifest," unless indeed where the result might do harm to others. And how could it be otherwise when we shall be freed from all the meanness, as well as from the grosser evil, of our Adam nature? And what meanness could be baser than to desire that everything which would bring us praise might be brought to light, but that all our faults and failings and sins might be concealed. Moreover, as Bengel beautifully puts it, "The everlasting remembrance of a great: debt which has been forgiven, will be the fuel of the strongest love."

And there is another element here involved, which our theology ignores. A Christian with the Bible in his hands does not need the well-accredited facts of Spiritualism to teach him that the denizens of the spirit world take notice of the acts of men. The declaration of God's righteousness in remitting sins committed prior to the death of Christ (Romans 3:25) was certainly not to satisfy the sinners whom He pardoned. It had reference, doubtless, to the high intelligences of heaven. For the salvation of fallen men is no "backstairs business." It will be in open view of all the angelic host that God will raise the sinners of the earth to heavenly glory. And may not the judgment of the bema of Christ have some reference to them? [3] And there is yet another consideration which is of such transcendent importance that it ought to silence every cavil. God has a purpose in our redemption, and that purpose is "the praise of the glory of His grace." Is it possible that anyone who knows anything of a true spiritual experience can believe, or even wish to believe, that ought will be concealed that tends to further that purpose? And there are two sides to this. Peter's denial of his Lord, and Demas "turning back in the day of battle," will be remembered there. But so will the widow's two mites, and Mary's alabaster box of ointment. It was in circumstances of trial such as we have never known that Demas and Peter failed. But who is there who has not failed at times when faithfulness would have cost nothing more than reproach or ridicule? And let us not forget that the widow's sacrifice would have been unrecorded had not the Lord been present to notice it; and that, but for Him, the reproach of "Why this waste" would have rested upon Mary. And in that day surely we shall have the grace to rejoice when service which brings honour from men will be appraised at its true worth, and many a humble Christian will be rewarded for sacrifices that no eye but His has noticed, or that men have noticed only to condemn.

3] I find that Bishop Wordsworth makes a suggestion of this kind in him commentary on the passage.

A forgotten truth it is indeed, this of the bema of Christ. And the wish to get rid of it is a grave reflection upon the Christianity of our own times. If we are to "have confidence, and not to be ashamed before Him at His coming," (1 John 2:28) it behooves us, instead of ignoring truth - which makes us ashamed here and now, to judge both heart and conduct in the light of it. The Christian who has an expurgated version of 2 Corinthians, from which the judgment-seat of Christ has been eliminated, would do well to turn his attention next to the following solemn words in Colossians - "Knowing that of the Lord ye shall receive the reward of the inheritance for ye serve the Lord Christ. But he that doeth wrong shall receive for the wrong which he hath done' and there is no respect of persons." [4]

4] To cite a case of another kind, will nothing be heard in that day of the evil work of Christian advocates of the Higher Criticism apostasy, by whom many a Christian life is wrecked, and multitudes of young Christians are stumbled? (Matthew 18:6.)

CHAPTER 12

EVANGELIZATION OF THE WORLD

THE exegetical system of "old-fashioned orthodoxy," "received by tradition from the Fathers," I once again repeat, leaves the Bible an easy prey to the sceptical attacks of the "Higher Criticism." In view of that movement, the defence of the Bible on the old lines is as hopeless as it would be to meet modern ordnance with the weapons which won the battle of Waterloo! If, for example, we persist in regarding the present Christian dispensation as the last aeon of God's dealings with mankind, and in ignoring Israel's place in the Divine counsels and purposes, the numerous eschatological passages in the Gospels and Epistles seem to be a tissue of wholly irreconcilable predictions. And an attempt to harmonize them serves only to bring their utter incongruity into stronger relief. And the clear and fearless thinker is thus tempted to jettison belief in the Divine inspiration of the Scriptures.

One of the saddest effects of this sceptical crusade is that, under its evil influence, the writings of Christian expositors are often as profane as those of avowed rationalists. Here, for example, is a sentence culled at random from the most recent Commentary of this school. Referring to the events predicted in Matthew 24:34, the writer says, "Jesus was quite certain that they would happen within the then living generation." [1]

> 1] The Expositor's Greek Testament. Dean Alford's Commentary tells us that the word here rendered generation has the meaning of a race or family of people.

To the Christian it is "quite certain" that the Lord Jesus was the Son of God, and that His words were the words of God — words that shall never pass away. Just as a spiritually devout Roman Catholic may be a true believer in Christ, though clinging to belief in the Virgin Mary and the saints, so these "critics" may unfeignedly believe in the deity of Christ; but in freely acknowledging this, we pay homage, not to their intelligence, but to their piety.

A well-taught child could understand what seems to be hidden from the wise and prudent of this kenosis theology. For the study of God's recorded dealings with His people, from Eden to Pentecost, will teach us that no Divine promise of blessing is ever marred by words to indicate the Divine foreknowledge that it will be rejected. At the beginning of His ministry, therefore, the Lord proclaimed that His kingdom was at hand, albeit, in this twentieth century of the Christian era, His people are still praying that it may come. And so also when, at the close of His ministry, He warned His people of the events that "must first come," He still spoke of it as near at hand; for He had in view the Pentecostal amnesty so soon to be proclaimed.

The First Gospel does not contain a single word that is inconsistent with its scope and purpose in the Divine scheme of revelation, as a record of the Lord's mission and ministry as Israel's Messiah; and it will be studied by believing Israelites in days to come as if the present Christian dispensation had never intervened. And on account of their ignoring this, some Christians suppose that the world must be evangelized before the return of Christ. It is "the gospel of the kingdom" that the Lord specified in His words in that connection, and "the end" to which He pointed is that of the age which will be brought to a close by His coming as Son of Man. At a missionary meeting long ago, when Charles Simeon sat down after speaking on behalf of missions to the Jews, Edward Bickersteth, the Secretary of the Church Missionary Society, put a penciled note into his hand, with the question, "8,000,000 Jews, 800,000,000 heathen — which is the more important?" To which Simeon promptly penciled the reply: "But what if the 8,000,000 Jews are to be 'life from the dead' to the 800,000,000 heathen?"

Although so plainly stated in Scripture, it is a forgotten truth that the full and final evangelization of the world awaits the restoration of Israel. And "the receiving" of Israel is necessarily deferred until after the coming of Christ to bring the present dispensation to a close. A forgotten truth, I call it, for in common with the "mystery" truths of the distinctively Christian revelation, it was lost in the interval between the Apostolic age and the era of the Patristic theologians. And our standard theology is so dominated by the writings of the Fathers that it is still unillumined by the light of the Evangelical Revival.

It may be remarked in passing that if the leaders in that revival had waited for the "Christian Church" to promote missions to the heathen, the heathen would possibly be still in midnight darkness. When, a few years before he sailed for India, William Carey rose in an assembly of Ministers of his own communion, to plead the cause he held so dear, he was peremptorily silenced as a troublesome fanatic. And the Church Missionary Society was the offspring of the despised and hated "Clapham Sect." The meeting at which it was founded was not held in either Westminster Abbey or St. Paul's, but in a small hired room in a poor sort of City inn. It was not till forty years afterwards that the ecclesiastical dignitaries accorded it their patronage. [2]

> 2] The history of the C.M.S. might save us from the baneful superstitions about "the Christian Church" which are so prevalent, and which are the great hindrance to a spiritual revival today. (See chap. 9., ante, especially pp. 97 ff.) These superstitions are opposed to the XXXIX Articles. See Canon Eden's Churchman's Theological Dictionary on Art. XIX, p. 87.

A brief recapitulation of the argument and contents of the preceding pages may fitly bring this final chapter to a close. If the sham "Higher Criticism" gains acceptance with Christians, it is certainly not because of the infidel element which permeates its teaching. Its success is due to prevalent ignorance of the distinctive truths of the Christian revelation. Redemption and forgiveness of sins through the blood of Christ, justification by faith, the resurrection of the dead and eternal judgment - these and other kindred truths are not Christian in any exclusive sense they are in the warp and woof of the Divine religion of Judaism. And we need not doubt that they pertained to the primeval revelation which preceded the call of Abraham. For one of the great purposes of that "call" was that the oracles of God, which men had corrupted, might be entrusted to the Covenant people. [3]

> 3] The Babylonian cult, which the "Higher Critics" regard as the source from which the cult of the Pentateuch was evolved, was the traditional and corrupt phase of that primeval revelation.

And although that people were often made subject to Gentile rule, first in the Servitudes, and again during all the centuries which followed the Babylonian conquest, yet, from Genesis to Malachi, there is nothing in Scripture to suggest that they would ever lose their privileged position as the people of God. Their being "cast off" was a crisis unparalleled since the call of Abraham — a crisis which, as we have seen, was a New Testament "mystery." And yet, in spite of the Apostle's warning, the exponents of Christendom religion are so "wise in their own conceits" that they not only regard the result as a matter of course, but in effect they accept the figment that God "has cast away His people whom He foreknew." But the intelligent Christian rejoices in the knowledge that "the gifts and calling of God are without repentance," and that Israel is yet to be restored to Divine favour, and to regain their normal place of privilege and testimony. And the "mysteries" of the Christian revelation are truths relating to the present abnormal economy of Israel's rejection.

No error is more common than that of supposing that the position from which the Jew has been dispossessed is now assigned to the Gentile. Gentiles, as such, whether professing Christians or pagan idolaters, share with Jews the common doom of sinful men. But "God has concluded them all under sin in order that He might have mercy upon all." For He to whom all judgment has been committed is now exalted as Saviour, and the Divine throne has thus become a throne of grace; "grace is reigning through righteousness unto eternal life."

But it is not merely as lost sinners that Jew and Gentile stand upon the same level. As believers in the Lord Jesus Christ both are raised to the same heavenly glory, and the same relationship as members of His Body. As the reign of grace is the basal "mystery," so this is the crowning "mystery" of the Christian revelation.

We have seen, however, that these "mysteries" are wholly incompatible with the special position and peculiar privileges Divinely accorded to Israel by the Abrahamic covenant. And this being so, the restoration of that people, so plainly foretold in Scripture, involves as definite a change of dispensation, as that which ushered in the present economy. And thus we are prepared for another "mystery," namely the Coming of the Lord, which will bring this economy to a close; and which, by calling His heavenly people home to heaven, will clear the way for the restoration of His earthly people to their normal position under the covenant. The "mystery" of the Coming is indeed a forgotten truth. And yet, apart from its influence on Christian life and character, no truth is more important in our defence of Scripture against the "learned ignorance" of the "Higher Criticism." For it is the pivotal truth of New Testament eschatology; and in the light of it — to change the figure — we can find perfect harmony in the teaching of the Gospels and Epistles on the subject of the Advent, where the sceptics see nothing but confusion. And lastly, the truth of the judgment-seat of Christ has received prominence in these pages. Even if Scripture were silent on this subject, a true spiritual instinct might teach a Christian to refuse the belief, which indeed the light of nature would lead us to reject, that when "we pass within the veil" all memories of earth will be effaced, and that as regards our future it is a matter of no practical importance whether we are faithful or unfaithful to the Lord. A revolt against such a false belief has betrayed very many into letting slip the truth that eternal life is a gift assured by Divine grace to all who come to Christ.

Others fall back upon the old heresy of a purgatory of some kind; though with pharasaical blindness they assume that the better sort of Christian will escape the fiery discipline. Others again, ignoring the "mysteries" both of grace and of the Coming, would have us believe that, although 1 Corinthians 15:51 assures us that at the Coming of the Lord we shall ALL be changed and called to heaven, those who have failed to attain some undefined standard of saintship will be punished by being left behind to await a later resurrection. And the newest and strangest theory of this class is that erring Christians, though destined to enjoy an eternity of heavenly glory, are to be denied a share in the millennial kingdom upon the earth. [4] But in marked contrast with all such vagaries of exegesis, the teaching of Scripture is clear. We are saved by grace through faith, and that (salvation) is not of ourselves, it is the gift of God, not of works lest any man should boast. (Ephesians 2:8, 9) And for the elect of this dispensation, salvation includes the resurrection and the glory. In this respect, therefore, the least worthy stands upon the same level with the most worthy of His people. But the judgment-seat of Christ will deal with every question which these human expedients are designed to solve.

4] See NOTE at the end of this Chapter.

In words as profoundly true as they are simple, the Westminster Divines have taught us that "Man's chief end is to glorify God and to enjoy Him for ever." And this end will be realized when the redeemed of earth shall stand in heavenly glory, the whole record of their past having been laid bare before Him who "died for their sins according to the Scriptures." And every attribute of God — not merely His grace and love, but His holiness and righteousness — will be so displayed and vindicated that the unfallen of heaven will unite with the redeemed of earth in ascriptions of eternal praise.

But the chief burden of these pages is the truth of the Lord's Coming. This subject is too often treated as a mere bypath of Christian doctrine. My aim has been to show that it is not merely the true hope of the Christian life, but that it is of such central importance in the New Testament revelation that ignorance or neglect of it leaves the Scriptures open to sceptical attack. And I have suggested that the seeming failure of the promise may be explained by the apostasy of Christendom, and the unfaithfulness of the people of God within the Professing Church. The great fact which claims our most earnest attention is that in Apostolic days the Christians were Divinely taught to look for the Lord's return as a present hope, and yet that it is still unfulfilled in this twentieth century of the Christian era. It is a fact which tries the faith of the believer, and supplies the sceptic with a plea for his unbelief.

It may be said, perhaps, that the Lord's promise that He would come "quickly" must be read in the light of the truth that with God "a thousand years are as one day." This I have already dealt with. And let us remember that these words are the complement of the other statement, "that one day is with the Lord as a thousand years." That is to say, time is not an element with Him in working out His purposes; and therefore all that these many centuries of the Christian era will bring of glory to Christ, and of blessing to us, might have been attained without this long delay. And this consideration should quiet the fears and solve the difficulties of any who think that a shortening of the Christian age would have clashed with the truth of the Body of Christ, and of our election to that position of glory. The promise of the Coming is identified with that very truth. And to say that, were it not for this two thousand years' delay, God could not have fulfilled all His purposes to usward, is a flagrant denial of the very truth upon which the above noticed objection is based.

These well-intentioned efforts to defend Divine truth by searching into the "unsearchable counsels" of God savour of Uzzah's fault in putting forth his hand to protect the ark. [5] And in these days of eager thought and earnest scepticism, it is perilous in the extreme to suggest that when the Lord declared He would come quickly, He meant that He would come in two thousand years! If this be so, then let us treat the promise as a secret to be spoken of in whispers, and only when no unbelievers are within earshot. For it would lead the profane to rejoice; and many a reverent and earnest seeker after truth would be stumbled and repelled. "What should we think of a fellow-man (they might exclaim) who makes a plain statement in simple words which he knows will be accepted everywhere in their ordinary acceptation, while he is using them in a mystical sense that entirely destroys their meaning!" [6]

> 5] It was a kindred misuse of the truth of the Divine counsels which led "the Christian Church" to oppose the pioneers of Gospel work in heathendom. We need a "Calvin Society" to clear that great teacher's name from the reproach of "Calvinism"!

6] There is no doubt as to the meaning of the words, viz. that He would come "quickly, speedily, without delay" (Grimm's Lexicon). The gloss, that when He does come He will come suddenly, is a sorry quibble. I may add, it is a glaring misuse of 2 Peter 3:8 to apply it here at all; and that not only because of the reason stated on p. 84, ante but also because the Lord here speaks in His human name, as when He taught by the Sea of Galilee, or at the Last Supper — "I Jesus... I am coming quickly." The mystery deepens when we realize that, if this strange hypothesis be true, the Lord's inspired Apostles were misled by His words. And it becomes overwhelming when we mark the care with which He warned His Jewish disciples in relation to His returning as Son of Man, that he would not come quickly.

The only adequate answer to this taunt is a repudiation of the suggestion which gives rise to it.

And if, rejecting that suggestion, we fall back upon the alternative offered in the preceding pages, we can plead the teaching of Scripture, from Eden to Patmos, that whenever Divine purposes or words have seemed to fail, the failure has been due to human sin, and almost always to the sin or unfaithfulness of the people of God. And we may plead also that, if this alternative solution of the difficulty be erroneous, the error is not one that can give occasion to the unbeliever to cavil at the faithfulness or truth of our Lord and Saviour. Every other word, without exception, that comes from His Divine lips is received by us with simple and unquestioning faith; let us accord a like faith to the promise of His Coming.

NOTE CHAPTER 12: EXCLUSION FROM MILLENNIAL KINGDOM

EXCLUSION from the millennial kingdom, we are told by some, will be the penalty imposed on Christians who lapse into immoral practices. And in proof of this we are referred to such passages as 1 Corinthians 6:9, 10; Galatians 5:21; Ephesians 5:5; etc. This assumes, however, that "the Kingdom of God" is merely a synonym for the millennial kingdom, an error which is exposed by the very first passage in which the phrase occurs in the Epistles. In Romans 14:17 we read, "The Kingdom of God is not meat and drink; but righteousness, and peace, and joy in the Holy Ghost." This reminds us of the Lord's words to Nicodemus.

The world and its religion is the natural sphere, but the Kingdom of God is spiritual; and none can enter it, none can see it, without a new birth by the Spirit. This is a truth of present and universal application. 1 Corinthians 15:50, which refers to the future, is a still more decisive refutation of the error. There we read that "flesh and blood cannot inherit the Kingdom of God"; that is, can have no place or part in it. But, as we all know, "flesh and blood" — men in their natural bodies — will be in the millennial kingdom.

Then again we recall the exhortation of 1 Thessalonians 2:12, "that ye would walk worthy of God, who hath called you unto His kingdom and glory." This is explained by Thessalonians 1:5, "that ye may be counted worthy of the Kingdom of God" — a reference not to the future state, but to the place and calling of the Christian here and now. It is akin to the exhortations of Ephesians 4:1 (R.V.), "I beseech you to walk worthily of the calling wherewith ye were called." For it is a present truth, and a fact of practical import, that the Christian has been "translated into the kingdom of the Son of His love" (Colossians 1:13). As a matter of fact, it is extremely doubtful whether the millennial kingdom is ever referred to in these Epistles of the Apostle Paul.

This scheme of exegesis, moreover, would teach us to acknowledge an "evil liver" as a Christian. But as 2 Timothy 2:19 tells us, the Divine seal has two faces: "The Lord knoweth them that are His" is the Godward side of it; the other, which is to govern our action, is "Let everyone that nameth the name of Christ depart from iniquity." But, we are told, the "incestuous person" in Corinth was a Christian. The inspired Apostle so decided; but to us it is not given to read the Godward face of the Divine seal, and we are bound to judge others by their profession and conduct. To acknowledge as a Christian any one who is living in open sin is to be false to the Lord. Our responsibility is to act on 1 Corinthians 6:9, 10 and similar Scriptures. But if every penitent has a claim upon Christian sympathy, surely one whom we have regarded as a fellow believer ought to be treated with unbounded patience and pity and Christian love. And let us not forget that there are sins more heinous than immoral acts. Some of the "unfortunates" of the streets may be nearer the kingdom than are men of high repute in the Professing Church, who are patterns of all virtue, but who deny the Deity and atoning work of the Lord Jesus Christ (Matthew 21:31). The doom of Sodom will be more tolerable than that of devout Capernaum (Matthew 11:23, 24).

What do the writers I am criticizing mean by "reigning with Christ"? Are all the many millions of the elect to sit on separate thrones? The Lord's words in Matthew 19:28 are clear. And some commentators refer to those words as explaining the first clause of Revelation 20:4. But is it not equally clear that in the latter clause, as in Romans 5:17 and 2 Timothy 2:12, the word is used in the secondary sense of "living royally" with Christ, or (as Grimm gives it) "to denote the supreme dignity, liberty, blessedness, which will be enjoyed by the redeemed "? And thus the word will be fulfilled for all; unless indeed we are to jettison the truth of grace, and make our heavenly calling and its blessings depend on merit. Certain it is that some will have special honours and rewards; but this truth does not conflict with the other.

In this closing section of the Apocalypse there is no element of historic fulfillment. The scheme I am criticizing assumes that "the first resurrection" is that of the "Coming" of Paul's Epistles: to me it seems certain that it is called "the first," with reference to the general resurrection of the 5th verse. And the language of verse 4 clearly indicates that it is the victims of the Tribulation who will have part in the first resurrection; for the redeemed of the present dispensation will have already passed to heaven in fulfillment of 1 Corinthians 15:51, 52. And it is not a matter of opinion, but of faith based on the Divinely-given words, that at that Coming of Christ none of His people will be left behind — "we shall not all sleep, but we shall ALL be changed."

Instead of accepting any of these theories, albeit they are suggested by a true spiritual instinct, let us seek to realize the responsibilities of our life on earth in view of the supreme solemnities of the judgment-seat of Christ.

THE END

www.ingramcontent.com/pod-product-compliance
Lightning Source LLC
Chambersburg PA
CBHW020425010526
44118CB00010B/421